SPIRITUAL
PERCEPTION

KEYS TO THE KINGDOM SERIES
POCKET EDITION

THIS BOOK SHOULD NOT BE LEFT
ACCESSIBLE, IN CLEAR VIEW, OR
SHARED CASUALLY WITH OTHERS

Published from
Mardukite Borsippa HQ, San Luis Valley, Colorado
Mardukite Academy & Systemology Society
for spiritual or philosophical purposes only

SPIRITUAL
PERCEPTION

Systemology
Advanced Training Course
Manual #6

As presented by Joshua Free
to the Systemology Society

THE JOSHUA FREE IMPRINT
JFI PUBLICATIONS

© 2024, JOSHUA FREE

ISBN : 978-1-961509-53-5

This manual is restricted to students on
The Systemology Advanced Training Course
that have already completed the
"Pathway to Ascension" Professional Course

References to prerequisite material:
Processing-Levels 0 to 6 (PC-1 to 16)
"The Secret of Universes" (AT #1)
"Games, Goals & Purposes" (AT #2)
"The Jewel of Knowledge" (AT #3)
"Implanted Universes" (AT #4)
"Entities and Fragments" (AT #5)

Review this prerequisite material:
PC Lesson-5 *"Free Your Spirit"*
PC Lesson-10 *"Lifting The Veils"*

Full use of this manual may also require:
"Systemology Biofeedback"
"Systemology Procedures" and
"Systemology Piloting"

First Edition Pocket Paperback — *March 2024*

mardukite.com

The Keys to the Kingdom are Yours for the Taking!

The official Mardukite Systemology "Advanced Training Course" is now available in print for the first time.

Those Seekers that have completed the "Pathway to Ascension" Systemology Professional Course can now access the upper-level teachings of our tradition.

This book is not for everyone…
This is the second manual for Level-8.

Never before has Joshua Free presented this material outside the confines of the Mardukite NexGen Systemology Society.

Learn how to expertly apply our spiritual technology toward reaching higher levels of Awareness and Beingness than ever before thought possible for humanity on planet Earth.

Each of the "Keys to the Kingdom" Advanced Training Course Manuals will further a Seekers reach on the Pathway leading out of this Universe.

The Pathway to Ascension Professional Course

#1 – *Increasing Awareness (Level-0)*
#2 – *Thought & Emotion (Level-0)*
#3 – *Clear Communication (Level-0)*
#4 – *Handling Humanity (Level-1)*
#5 – *Free Your Spirit (Level-2)*
#6 – *Escaping Spirit-Traps (Level-2)*
#7 – *Eliminating Barriers (Level-3)*
#8 – *Conquest of Illusion (Level-3)*
#9 – *Confronting the Past (Level-4)*
#10 – *Lifting the Veils (Level-4)*
#11 – *Spiritual Implants (Level-5)*
#12 – *Games and Universes (Level-5)*
#13 – *Spiritual Energy (Level-6)*
#14 – *Spiritual Machinery (Level-6)*
#15 – *The Arcs of Infinity (Level-6)*
#16 – *Alpha Thought (Level-6)*

Keys to the Kingdom Advanced Training

#1 – *The Secret of Universes (Level-7)*
#2 – *Games, Goals & Purposes (Level-7)*
#3 – *The Jewel of Knowledge (Level-7)*
#4 – *Implanted Universes (Level-7)*
#5 – *Entities & Fragments (Level-8)*
#6 – *Spiritual Perception (Level-8)*
#7 – *Mastering Ascension (Level-8)*
#8 – *Advancing Systemology (Level-8)*

Systemology Biofeedback
Systemology Procedures
Systemology Piloting

TABLET OF CONTENTS

Advanced Manuals should be studied in the sequential order in which they are numbered.

INTRODUCTION TO THE MANUAL

This manual is restricted to students on
The Systemology Advanced Training Course
that have already completed the
"Pathway to Ascension" Professional Course

References to prerequisite material:
"The Secret of Universes" (AT #1)
"Games, Goals & Purposes" (AT #2)
"The Jewel of Knowledge" (AT #3)
"Implanted Universes" (AT #4)
"Entities and Fragments" (AT #5)
Processing-Levels 0 to 6 (PC-1 to 16)

Review this prerequisite material:
PC Lesson-5 *"Free Your Spirit"*
PC Lesson-10 *"Lifting The Veils"*

THE SYSTEMOLOGY ADVANCED TRAINING COURSE MANUAL SERIES

Mardukite Systemology is a new evolution in Human understanding about the "systems" governing *Life*, *Reality*, the *Universe* and all *Existences*. It is also a *Spiritual Path* used to transcend the Human experience and reach *"Ascension."*

This is an *Advanced Training* (*AT*) course manual detailing *upper-levels* of our spiritual philosophy. It is intended to assist *advancing* a *Seeker's* personal progress toward the *upper-most levels* of the *Pathway*.

This manual follows after our *Professional Course* series of lessons—available as individual booklets, or collected in two volumes titled *"The Pathway to Ascension"* The *Professional Course* follows after material given in the *Basic Course* booklets, or *"Fundamentals of Systemology"* volume.

The systematic methodology that we use to assist an individual to increase their *"Actualized Awareness"* (and reach gradually higher toward their *"Spiritual Ascension"*) is referred to as *"The Pathway"* — and that individual is called a *"Seeker."*

To receive the greatest benefit from this manual: it is expected that a *Seeker* will already be familiar with the fundamental concepts and terminology (previously relayed in the *Basic Course* and *Professional Course* lessons) of our *applied philosophy.*

As a *Seeker* increases their *Awareness* in this lifetime, their spiritual *"Knowingness"* also increases—which is to say their *certainty* on *Life,* on this and other *Universes,* and on *realizing Self* as an unlimited "spiritual being" *having* an enforced restrictive "human experience." A *Seeker* also *knowingly* increases their command and control of the "human experience." And this is a part of what is meant by *"Actualized Awareness."*

CHARTING FLIGHTS ON THE PATHWAY

Although there is a systematic structure to *fragmentation*, the personal journey experienced along the *Pathway* will be different for each *Seeker*. For example, certain areas will seem more *"turbulent"* or difficult for one *Seeker* than another. We tend to say that these areas have more *"charge"* on them—or that they are more *"heavily charged."* It is best to handle such areas when you are already feeling "good" and not in a situation (or condition) where that specific area is consistently being *"triggered"* or *"restimulated."*

As an applied philosophy, *Systemology* "theory" can be easily utilized in the "laboratory" of the "world-at-large" in everyday life. This is implied within the basic instruction of each lesson. Unlike other "sciences" that conduct experiments by making a change to some "objective variable" *out there* and waiting to see an effect, our focus is the individual (or *Observer*) themselves, and how *they* affect the "*Reality*" perceived.

Our philosophy is applied by using specific exercises and systematic techniques. These "*processes*" provide the most stable personal gain (and *realizations*) for each area; but only when actually applied with a *Seeker's* full "*presence*" and *Awareness*. Hundreds of such *processes* may be found in the "*Pathway to Ascension*" (*Professional Course*) material.

Applying a technique is called "*running a process*." *Processes* are designed with very simple instructions or "*command-lines*." To *run* a *processing command-line*, a *Seeker* may be assisted by the communication of that *line* from a "*Co-Pilot*" (as in "*Traditional Piloting*"). But even then, a *Seeker* must still personally "input" the *command* as *Self*. For this reason—and quite thankfully—*Solo-Processing* is possible.

TAKING FLIGHT ON THE PATHWAY

Processing Techniques are intended to treat the *Spiritual Being* or *Alpha-Spirit*; the individual themselves. The *"command-lines"* are *directed to* the individual themselves—not some *mental machinery* of theirs, and not even a *Biofeedback* metering device.

Systematic Processing is applied by the *Alpha-Spirit*—who then *Self-directs* command of their "Mind-System" or "body" (*genetic-vehicle*), both of which are "constructs" that the *Alpha-Spirit* (*Self*, or the "I-AM" *Awareness unit*) operates, but neither of which is actually *Self*. *Fragmentation* causes *Humans* to falsely identify *Self as* the "*Mind*" or even a "*Body.*"

Some *processes* can be treated quite lightly at first; others may require a bit of working at in order to get "*running*" well. It is important to set aside a period of time when you can be dedicated to your studies and *processing*. This period of time is referred to as a *"processing session."* When a *process* does start *running* well, it is important to be able to complete it to a satisfactory *"end-point."*

Processing allows us to be able to *actually* "look" at *things* and even determine the *considerations* we have made—or attitudes we have decided—about *Reality* as a result of those experiences.

It doesn't do us much good to simply "glance"—or to *restimulate* something uncomfortable and then quickly *withdraw* from it once again, leaving more of our *attention* yet again behind and held fixedly on it.

Generally speaking, a *Seeker* continues to *run* a *process* so long as something is "happening"—which is to say, the *process* is still producing a change. Usually this is evident by the type of "answers" that a *command-line* prompts a *Seeker* to originate from the database of their own *Mind-System*.

Processing Command-Lines ("PCL") are not "magic words"; they do not "do" anything on their own. They systematically assist a *Seeker* to direct their own attention toward increasing *Awareness*.

A *Seeker* may also cease to generate new "data" from a *process* without reaching an *"ultimate" realization* as an *"end-point."* It is possible that additional "layers" (or even other "areas") require handling before anything "deeper" is accessible. If this is the case, end the *process.* But, if a *Seeker* is *withdrawing* from something uncomfortable that was incited or stirred up, then a *process* is *run* until they feel "good" about it.

One of the benefits to *Flying-Solo* on the *Pathway* is that the *processing* is entirely *Self-determined.* This naturally provides a certain built-in "safety" for a practitioner. Anything you *restimulate* by *Self-determinism* is *your thing*. It is not triggered or incited by some external "*other-determined*" influences (or other "source-points") that make you an *effect*. It can be more easily handled in *processing* — or you can simply let things "cool down" and come back to it again in another *session*.

While it may seem "mysterious" to beginners, a *Seeker* gets a sense for knowing how long to *run* a *process* only with practice. Once you have spent some time actually applying material from "*The Pathway to Ascension*" *Professional Course*, there are many aspects of it that become "second nature" because they are, in fact, a part of our true original native nature. All we have done in *Systemology* is "*reverse engineer*" the routes of *creation* and *consideration* that are already *our own*.

SYSTEMOLOGY LEVEL-8

We are publishing *"upper-level" Systemology* in *2024* for the very first time. Its effective application is dependent on a *Seeker* having already reached a stable point of *"Beta-Defragmentation."* This requires proper use of materials for *processing-levels 0 to 6*—as given in the *"Pathway to Ascension" Professional Course* (available in two volumes, or sixteen individual booklets).

Additionally, this current *Systemology Level-8* work is a direct continuation of *Level-7*, which *must* be completed before continuing. The *Systemology Level-7* manuals—*"The Secret of Universes,"* *"Games, Goals & Purposes,"* *"The Jewel of Knowledge"* and (to a lesser extent) *"Implanted Universes"*—should be treated as a single "unit" of work *prior* to approaching *Level-8*. These manuals are available individually, or as collected in *Volume One* of the *"Keys to the Kingdom" Advanced Training (A.T.) Course.*

After uncovering *"The Jewel"* and discovering the "secret" of *Universes*, a *"Seeker"* has *found* the "hidden gem" of the *Pathway* at *Level-7*, and is no longer a *"Seeker."* Of course, things are not always what we expect—and *"all that glitters is not gold."* Yet, still, it is *"The Jewel of Knowledge"* (*Parts #1-5*) and the *Entry-Point Heaven Incident*, *&tc.*, that represents the "ceiling" of *this Universe* and even what is behind it, beneath it, or embedded into its structure. It was what a *"Seeker"* had been *drawn* to in their *search*, but was never meant to find by any other method or avenue, except *systematically*.

Systematology Level-8 is the first official *"Wizard Level"* of the *Systemology Society*. As stated in *A.T. Manual #4*: while "formal" *Advanced Training* may end with manuals representing *Systemology Level-8* (and completing the "*Keys to the Kingdom*" series), this will also open up, what is referred to by the *Mardukite Academy* as, the "*Infinity Grade*." [For instructional purposes, we tend to still refer to a practitioner as a "*Seeker*" in the *upper-level* manuals.]

There is no finite end-point to the "*Infinity Grade*" because its ultimate goal is the "*increase of spiritual perception*," which is, in essence, *unlimited*. This means that plenty of room remains for future researchers to contribute; but only after first completing their *Advanced Training* regarding the parts of our "*Map*" that are *already* researched, well-plotted, effective in application, and thus published.

A *Seeker* could complete *A.T. Manual #3*, and then move on directly to *Level-8* with *A.T. Manual #5* ("*Entities & Fragments*"). If, however, a *Seeker* doesn't have enough "*reality*" on that *Level-8* material—as in, it

doesn't seem *"real"* enough to them—
then some time studying *A.T. Manual #4*
(*"Implanted Universes"*) may be of benefit.
The covert purpose of introducing *"Implant Platforms #1-18"* (*AT#3*) and the
"IPU Platforms" (*AT#4*) at *Level-7,* is really
to make *"Entities & Fragments"* (*AT#5*)
more accessible.

To apply *upper-level Systemology,* an *advanced Seeker* must follow the prescribed
outline of instruction that is now available for the first time to the public as the
"Keys to the Kingdom" series.

Advanced Manuals should be studied in the sequential order in which they are numbered.

A.T. MANUAL #6
SPIRITUAL
PERCEPTION

Keep these prerequisite materials accessible:
Processing-Levels 0 to 6 (PC-1 to 16)
"The Secret of Universes" (AT #1)
"Games, Goals & Purposes" (AT #2)
"The Jewel of Knowledge" (AT #3)
"Implanted Universes" (AT #4)
"Entities and Fragments" (AT #5)

Review this prerequisite material:
PC Lesson-5 "Free Your Spirit"
PC Lesson-10 "Lifting The Veils"

ADVANCING SPIRITUAL ABILITY

This book is a *systematic training manual*; it is *not* a complete record of *all* experimental research or potential commentary on the subjects included (which would require many volumes). The author spent *30* years dedicated to *"spiritual cartography,"* exploring every potential avenue —from the *most ancient* extant writings available, to the *New Thought* developments of the *20th Century*—before presenting this series of *Systemology* work. Only those "bits" truly useful for *crafting* the *ultimate map* for *The Way Out* were retained.

The ultimate freedom of *Self*—the *Alpha-Spirit*—*knowingly* operating "outside" (or *"exterior to"*) a mortal organic *Body* is our true basic spiritual state. It is the *rehabilitation* of this state—or an *actualized realiza-*

tion of it—that has driven the populations towards various philosophies, metaphysics, and religion, for thousands of years. Of course, various communication barriers and organizational corruption has kept any of these other "avenues" from fully delivering a *Seeker* to their desired *destination*.

The new standard *Systemology* program— *Basic Course, Professional Course* and *Advanced Training Course*—is the result of feedback from many *systemologists* over the course of many years. It didn't matter how well something *worked* or was *understood* by the author; the real test of its *effectiveness* was reaching a point of *perfection* for its *presentation*—where *Systemology* could be properly communicated to, and used by, others.

Unlike most other *"New Age"* pursuits: we took a *systematic* and *scientific* approach to *Life, Universes* and *Everything*— but while neither adopting, nor excluding, a *physically-mechanistic technological* viewpoint of understanding. The results were a *"spiritual technology"*—something *actually* useful to the *Alpha-Spirit*—that exceeds the boundaries of *this Life*, *the Human Condition*, and even *this Universe*.

Previous *spiritual* traditions sought to find a way out by *denying* or *altering* *"What Is."* But while *eastern mysticism* and *western magic* may have been successful in producing many various *effects*, not one of them produced the manifestation of a *True Map* for *The Way Out*.

Advanced Training procedures of this manual are only expected to be effective for those *Seekers* that have *actually processed through* the *"Pathway-to-Ascension" Professional Course* (*Lesson-1 to 16*) and the *"Keys to the Kingdom" A.T. Manuals* (*#1 to 5*) prior to studying/applying this manual (*AT #6*). This manual is combined with *"Entities & Fragments"* (*AT#5*) to function as a single unit of *"Level-8"* training.

[*AT#7* and *AT#8* are recent expansions to the *A.T.* course that encourage additional work and research for this *Infinity Grade.*]

Ideally, a *Seeker* handles what is initially accessible during *AT#5*, then completes a *"run through"* of *spiritual perception* development in *AT#6*. At that time, they may revisit the procedures in *AT#5* to check if there is anything newly accessible. Increased *spiritual perception* makes *releasing entities* (and *fragments, &tc.*) easier; and *releasing entities* makes techniques for increasing *spiritual perception* more effective.

"Free Your Spirit" (*PC-5*) and *"Lifting The Veils"* (*PC-10*) should be reviewed—and considered *"introductions"* to this manual. All other *Systemology* material should also be kept accessible. Many *advanced exercises* already given in previous lessons and manuals will be referenced directly —but their full background and instruction will not be repeated here, so more

ground can be covered in a shorter space for this manual.

A.T. Manual #6 is prepared with an expectancy that it will not require any *strenuous effort* (for a *Level-8 Seeker*) to understand or apply—however, *"repetitive practice"* is likely necessary. Most of the *exercises* will be presented with little theory or explanation attached—because a *Seeker* that has *actually* worked through *previous* material will already be familiar with many of the techniques and *processing*-types described here.

The original *Wizard Level-0 "Creative Ability Training"* procedure premiered in the *Systemology Core Research Volume: "Imaginomicon"* (in *2021*). These exercises were spread all over the new standard *Professional Course Processing-Levels 0 to 6* as *"objective-environment processing," "creativeness processing,"* and *"advanced techniques."* They were intentionally included to accelerate a *Seeker's* progress on the *Pathway*—and as preparation for *upper-level A.T.* work. Of course, at *those levels*, such exercises were treated quite lightly in between more intensive *defragmentation processing.*

A *Seeker* enters *Level-8* (as a *processing level*) at *Wizard Level-0*. It is at *this* level that *AT#5* (*Entities*) material is treated the *first* time through. Remaining *Wizard-Levels* pertain to theoretical *Infinity Grade "Arcs"*—leading further upward toward total *mastery of Ascension Technology*—most of which are in experimental stages of development, or still remain to be researched and realized.

The new *Wizard Level-1 "Advanced Ability Training Program"* (proposed in this manual) revisits many earlier *advanced techniques*—but also adds many more. This manual also includes a *Wizard Level-2* training procedure. When a *Seeker* approaches *AT#5* material a *second* time, they will be doing so from a *Wizard Level-1* (or higher) foundation or *viewpoint*. [An experimental *Wizard Level-3* routine appears in *AT#7.*]

"*End-point Realizations*" for *Wizard-Levels* primarily regard an increased sense of, and certainty in, *Self* as the *Alpha-Spirit*. "*Ability*" and "*certainty*" tend to be correlated. But this alone doesn't provide much of a *systematic* gradient. Any upward emphasis requires codification using our theoretical *Infinity-Grade* "*Arcs.*"

Wizard Level-1 : "*ejecting*" *Awareness* (*fixed viewpoint*) from the *Body*; handling the *Body* (from nearby) while operating from a *viewpoint* that is *remote* from (or "*exterior to*") any *Body*.

Wizard Level-2 : "*perceiving*" from *exterior viewpoints* that are *projected/ extended away/remote* from a *Body*.

Wizard Level-3 : "*intending*"; a proposed experimental gradient. [This level is still subject to future revision and includes material that may later be classified as a *"higher"* gradient of *Wizard-Level*.]

Most early *Systemology* research into procedures for this area was conducted during *experimental workshops* and *Traditional (Co-Piloted) Sessions*. Having a *Co-Pilot* allowed a *Seeker* to focus *attention* more on *"doing"* the *processing command-lines* (PCL) rather than *"thinking"* about book-instructions. A *Seeker* often felt "safer" handling *processing* "exterior to" a *Body* when the *session-environment* was properly controlled (*piloted*)—and without any distractions or chance of sudden disturbances.

However, *Co-Piloting "Advanced Ability Training"* is not without its complications. A *Level-8 Co-Pilot*, requires having some personal *reality* on these *processes* in order to effectively *guide* a *Seeker*. Otherwise, there is a greater risk of a *Co-Pilot* "*invalidating*" a *Seeker's* experiences, gains, and *abilities*. *Invalidation* results in having less *certainty*—which slows (or stops) progress with *Spiritual Perception*.

A *Co-Pilot* will *acknowledge* the *ejection*, but *never* makes the *Seeker* "*prove*" their *Beingness* (or *ability*) by producing any phenomenon, *&tc*. The standard practice was to simply continue the *process* that a *Seeker* "*ejected*" with, but from their current *viewpoint*.

However, since *ejection* can occur rather suddenly—and a sudden *shift* in *processing* can sometimes cause more *confusion*—this mainly applied to *objective exercises*. In addition to this, sometimes the *Seeker* found themselves suddenly "*looking at*" something else (*imagery, an incident, &tc.*), and so the alternative practice of making *copies* of that *imagery, &tc.,* was developed.

For example: if a *Seeker* is practicing "*Creation-Of-Space*" and suddenly gets a lot of certainty on operating from a *viewpoint* that is *exterior-to* a *Body*, then they would continue their "Creation-Of-Space" exercise from that *viewpoint*. But if that became distracting because the *Seeker* was now dealing with some other phenomenon, they would handle that by making/ create "copies" (*knowingly, intentionally*) of whatever it was they *did see*; making many copies of the *imagery*, then alternating "throwing them away" (or *dispersing* them) and "pushing them in" on the *Body*.

REALIZATIONS FROM THE PATHWAY

Shared Universes and *Games* are "*contrary*" or "*antithetical*" to the true basic native state (or even "*Home Universe*") of an *Alpha-Spirit*. Our highest level of *spiritual perception* and *ability* does not permit "*game-conditions*" to exist—does not allow for us to experience any kind of *Game*.

The *Alpha-Spirit* is *"Pure Awareness"*—
without *energetic-mass* or *location*—but it
has an unlimited potential for *postulating*,
creating, and even *considering* the condition of *"Having"* something. It can *be anywhere* it cares *to be; looking* at *anything* it
wants *to be looking* at.

But, in order to *have games*—*"game-fields"*
and *"enforced rules"*—*Alpha-Spirits* became expert specialists in *designing* and
creating various *barriers* and *restrictions*.

We have come to believe that *"something
is better than nothing"*—and it is only by
achieving high-tolerance levels that a
Seeker can rehabilitate the *"confronting of
Nothingness."* In addition to this, we must
rehabilitate *creativeness*—the certainty
that a *Seeker* can *still "Have"* something independent of a *Body*—or even the *Game*
of *this Physical Universe* altogether.
Without rehabilitating these basic states,
an individual will not let go, or release

Self, from their *chronic* and *compulsive participation* with the *Human Condition.*

Restoring *freedom* is synonymous with restoring *spiritual perception* and *ability.* But, *total freedom* does not have a *systematic structure,* because it is a *basic Truth*— reflecting the true native state of the *Alpha-Spirit.* The innate *abilities* of an *Alpha-Spirit* cannot actually be destroyed, because *It Is* the basic *Beingness* of its *Existence.* However, *consciously understanding* and/or *knowingly using* these *abilities* (and *perceptions*) can certainly become *fragmented* and *blocked.*

Freedom is the absence of *barriers* and *restriction.* "Total Freedom" would be the *total absence* of *all barriers* and *restriction.* The *Alpha-Spirit* has long since lost its tolerance for *confronting* such a state. At the upper-most level, there is *nothing* to be *free from.* That the "*something*" to be *free from,* is more or less an *illusion,* is also true; but it is the *Alpha-Spirit's* own *illu-*

sion—agreed to (at some level) in order to *have* a game. [Ref. *AT#1 & AT#2*]

Our *Awareness* is currently "spread" all over *this* and *other* "Universes"—"*attention-units*" *fragmented* by *imprinting*, "*splitting*" and other *incidents* where *attention* remains "*fixed*." *Fixation* is *entrapment*. All *fixation* is really the *suspension* of *Awareness* (*attention*) on a point of a "*communication-cycle*" that has not resolved, closed, or ended. It is *suspended* in a *confusion* or a "*maybe*." And this obviously reduces *Knowingness*.

Note that the phrase "*communication-cycle*" refers to more than "conversations" with other *people*; it also includes incomplete *cycles-of-action* (or "events" that we've experienced)—or really any "encounters" with the *energy-matter* and/or *space-time* of *this* (or any *other*) Universe.

An insistence upon substituting *Knowingness* by obsessively holding onto *imprin-*

ted imagery (*mental pictures*) in order to "learn by experience"—and then assigning *automatic control* of *associating* the *data* to *reactive-response machinery*—has inhibited the *total freedom* of the *Alpha-Spirit*.

Spiritual Perception is really only inhibited and limited by one key factor:

What—and how much—an Alpha-Spirit is willing to Know.

The *perception* of *freedom* is connected to:

What an Alpha-Spirit is willing to Create, Do, or Have.

And this is where an individual got themselves involved with the *games* and *puzzles* that an *Alpha-Spirit* is so fond of. Unless a *Seeker* has *certainty* on the *ability* to *Create* another (preferably better) "*game*"—or at the very least *Have* one —"*somewhere*" else, they will not sufficiently *release* their *hold* on "*this*" one.

Systematic Processing on the *Pathway* has

established to a *Seeker* that our true basic native *ability* is restored by *Knowingness*— the increase of *Actualized Awareness*. The *unknowing* ("*not-conscious*") *automation* and "*push-button*" *mechanistic control* is a much *lower-level* of "*mental operation*" than *Knowingness*.

The "*Standard Model*" (and "*ZU-Line*") on which our *Systemology* is based, very accurately "maps" or "charts" the conditions of descent in any area. At the top we have:

7. ALPHA-THOUGHT—(*To Be*)—the *postulates* of *Creation*; *Creating* a "*thing*" to *Know* about.

6. KNOWINGNESS—(*What Is*)—the *condition* of *Knowing*; *Total-Knowingness* is all-pervasive perfect *Knowing* about a "*thing*" as maintained by its *Creator*.

5. INTENTION—(*It-As-Altered*)—the *ability* to affect or change the *condition*

of an *existing "thing"* to make it
continue, persist, or *perpetuate,* in some
way.

For there to be *"intention"* (rather than
"Creation") the *Alpha-Spirit* already must
have decided to *"Not-Know"* about something. The *intention* to *Know something*
requires *Not-Knowing* about it in the first
place. The *intention* to *"learn"* requires an
interest—and *"interest"* is something that
is difficult for an *Eternal Spirit* to maintain
indefinitely (hence, *"games"*). An individual in *Total Knowingness* would simply
disperse an *undesired "thing"* and *Create*
something else, rather than *Alter-What-Is.*

The extent to which one can *Imagine* (or
Create) does not only concern *Creating*
(*Imagining*) *"infinities"* of something (see
PC-15, &tc.), but also the *"distance-factor."*
Distance is another *perceived barrier* in
space-time. So, when *running* any type of
"creativeness processing," we must also
treat the matter of: how *"close"* does

one's *creations* have to be (to their *view-point*/POV) to still be *considered* (handled) under their *control?*

Lower down the chained-sequence: when operating with a *Body* in the *Human Condition*, the *Alpha-Spirit* typically directs *"intention"* to the *"Mind-System"* in order to get the *Body* to *"do"* things, in order to affect the *energetic-mass* of *space-time* in the *Game* of *this Physical Universe*. This involves a *consideration* that some kind of "action" or "effort" is required in order to *cause* something—and this part of the chain starts with:

4. THINKINGNESS—(*Computation*)—the *evaluation* of *effort* of some *"doingness"* to *Cause* or *Have* something; and/or the *estimation* of *control* (to *"start,"* *"alter,"* or *"stop"* an existing *system* or *"thing"*).

"Thinkingness" (the *Mind-System*) operates far below a level of *Knowingness*. It is unnecessary; it is where most *beings* get

themselves into trouble. Of course, to get to this point, a *being* would have to *Not-Know* about a lot of *created things* in order to *"think about things to know about."* But this is exactly what sets up the conditions for a *game*.

"EJECTION" FROM A BODY/VEHICLE
(*Wizard Level-1*)

The phrase *"ZU-Vision"* is used in *Systemology* to indicate the experience of the true *Spiritual Awareness* (and thus the *Spiritual Life*) of the *Alpha-Spirit*. This is beyond the *sensation* or *perception* of a *Body*; it is beyond the *mental machinery* and *fragmented computations* of any *Mind-System*.

ZU-Vision regards *Beingness* that is completely *"exterior to"* Body and Mind. Other methods and traditions that do not properly *defragment* a *Seeker* first, may occasionally get them *"out-of-body"* — but the individual is still very much *"in-the-mind"* and attached to all their "stuff" and their interconnection to *bodies* of *this Universe.*

Although it may seem to cross-over in subject matter at times: when handling *Spiritual Perception* at *Wizard Level-1*, we are not directly interested in what is often referred to as *"psychic phenomenon"* or making objective demonstrations of *ability* in *this Physical Universe.*

When unrestricting *fixed viewpoints* in *Space*, one is also treating *Time* — and at first, a *Seeker* may not have *clear "present-time" perception* with *ZU-Vision* on the immediate environment of the *Body*. One's *actual perception* must also be distinguished from the *"mental imagery"* that one is likely to still be *compulsively creating* (to *look at*). A *Seeker* may initially not *perceive* the *Physical Universe* because the *Seeker*, themselves, is not *"putting it up there to see."* [This strongly hints toward a very specific and significant *A.T. realization.*]

ZU-Vision is not a *process, procedure* or *skill.* It is the natural *ability* of an *Alpha-Spirit* that simply has varying degrees of *clarity in perception*—and thus, like any *ability* or *function,* it can be *inhibited* or *fragmented.* To treat this subject as a *process* directly would be like writing a book instructing on how to *"eat," "walk,"* or *"breathe"* (although such exist). There are obviously ways of "improving" how one does such things, but the basic development of the function is essentially *in-born* or *innate.*

Alpha-Spirits have developed a *compulsive dependency* on *bodies, automation,* and *games.* We can rehabilitate *Spiritual Perception* by resolving (*defragmenting*) the *compulsions.* This is the real emphasis of the *Pathway*—because any time we tried to directly focus *processing* specifically on "*getting out*," we encountered many *barriers*. Instead, initial gains were accomplished by *processing-out* the "*entry-points*"—the "*getting in*" part. Secondly, we achieved gains by *processing-out incidents* of unwanted or unexpected (*other-determined*, rather than *Self-Determined*) "*ejections*" from anything, but mostly *bodies*.

To effectively apply the techniques of *Wizard Level-1* as a *systematic procedure*, a *Seeker* must *Know* (have *actual* certainty on):

1. "*What*" *is* being *ejected/released* (the *Alpha-Spirit*);

2. "*What*" *it is* being *ejected/released* "*from*" (the *Body*); and

3. "*mechanisms/machinery*" (called the *Mind*).

Years of experimental research allowed us to collect data regarding key factors that more commonly affected *Seekers* experiencing difficulties with *ejecting/releasing* from their *Body*. Many of these points are treated earlier on the Pathway, but a *Seeker* may need to revisit key areas specific to their own case, or even other areas that may have yet to be personally handled at all, for *Wizard Level-1*. These include:

–FEAR associated with some element of *space-time, energy,* and/or *mass;* or else *terminals* attached to *this Universe.*

–FEAR associated with *lack* or *loss* of "having" *space-time* or *energy-mass;* including reduced *ability-to-confront* "Nothingness."

–NO RESPONSIBILITY (OR CONTROL); therefore the *effect of,* or *controlled by,* other things (*other-determinism*).

–NO CERTAINTY; low-*Awareness;* no *Self-Determinism,* therefore everything is *other-determined,* or from an *unknown (hidden) source.*

–MACHINERY; excessively burdened by

personal *mechanisms* of *automation* and *reactivity*.

–BEINGNESS (VIEWPOINT or POV) deeply enmeshed in the *rigid-energy* (*standing-waves*) of a *Body*; either a *fixation* on the *Body*, or total lack of interest/responsibility in handling the *Body* ("disowning" while still remaining connected to it).

–BEINGNESS (VIEWPOINT/POV) or ATTENTION fixedly on an entirely different *Body* (as a personal *identification*) than the *current Human Body* (*vehicle*) "present" *in-session*.

The last one is an interesting point of *fragmentation* only recently added to the list. In this case, we may have a situation of treating the "*wrong body.*" *Ejecting Awareness* from "*the Body*" actually re-quires the starting point of *being in* "*the Body*"—and preferably "*the Body*" being used for a *processing session* that keeps directing PCL regarding "*that Body.*" In the case of *wrong body*: it may be that an individual's chronic POV is on (or from) a *desired body*, or they have *fixated attention* on a *past body* (previous *body* on the *Backtrack*).

At *Level-8*, a *Seeker/Wizard* no longer *runs* "imprint-chains" in *processing*. The primary *high-level Awareness* methods of *processing* are: "Spotting" and "defragmentation-upon-analytical-inspection."

This means that basic "Recall" and "Imagine" techniques still apply, in addition to *identifying* "Source," "What Is," &tc. We don't want to *stick* a *Seeker's attention* on a *Body*, but *ejection* can be difficult if *attention* is already *fixated* on a *Body* "elsewhere." In this instance, more "descriptive"-style PCL may need to be *run* in order to "collect" one's "attention-units" onto the *current Body*. This sometimes means first getting a *Seeker* to *realize "what"* Body/ Identity they *actually* have their *Awareness/Beingness* associated with.

"What Body Would You Like To Have?"

–and/or–

"Describe Your Last Body."

As a preliminary to *Wizard Level-1 Procedure*, a *Seeker* should *defragment* prior "*other-determined*" *ejections* where *Awareness* may be suspended and/or new *considerations* may have been made about *being* "*exterior-to*" a *Body*. This includes, for example: *past deaths, serious illness*, or *injuries*—points when an *Alpha-Spirit* may have temporarily "*gone out*" of the *Body*, or was otherwise *ejected* "*under duress.*" [It has been noticed, on the *Backtrack*, that the *Alpha-Spirit* does not "naturally" recover full *attention-Awareness* after such *incidents.*]

There is a phenomenon where a *Seeker*/individual "*goes out*" (*ejects*) and "*goes back in*" (*snaps-in*) so quickly that the *shift* isn't fully *realized* as having happened; but the "*impact*" (of the "*snap-in*") is *perceived* in some way, which often results in a period of *confusion* (or some other unwanted manifestation). Prior use of *mysticism* or *occultism* (that included *astral travel* or *out-of-body experiences*) may need to be *de-fragmented*. Previous *processing-sessions*, where a *Seeker* may have suddenly *ejected*, might also require *"repair."*

The main issue is that these events often take place before *Seekers* are properly prepared to handle them. This leaves *residual fragmentation* from the subsequent *"snap-in"* effects thereafter. And any heightened *perception* achieved is generally not very stable. An unprepared *Seeker* may find the experience disorienting—or a disturbance occurs in the *session-environment* while they are operating *"exterior"*—and so they abruptly *snap-back-in*, and "hold on" even tighter to the *Human Condition*.

Early experiments placed particular emphasis on the *"getting out"* part of things. But few of the methods applied directly toward this goal actually produced stable results—or if they were effective in *knowingly ejecting Awareness*, the experience didn't leave a *Seeker* feeling much better, especially if something *caused them* to *snap-back-in*. [This was the case with most traditional applications of *"Astral Projection"* data.]

A.T. realizations include a greater certainty on *being* a *"Spiritual Being"*; *not* a *"Body"*—and that the *Alpha-Spirit* is a *Beingness* that can *consider* itself as *being* *"anywhere"* and *"anything."* The typical individual (*Alpha-Spirit + Human Condition*) generally *considers* that they *need* a *Body*, or that the *Body needs* them, or even that they would be *abandoning* it by *ejecting*.

At *Wizard Level-1* we are primarily concerned with *"ejection"* (and *defragmenting "snap-in"* effects). Our emphasis at this stage is not on vivid *perception*. First we *"get out"*; then we focus on *"looking around."* Upon initially *"getting out,"* a *Seeker* often *"loses"* the *perception* of *present-time environmental* "anchor-points" in the *Physical Universe*. Their *spiritual perception* is not likely to be "very good" (*clear*) without some kind of *"dimension-points."* This is remedied by practicing *"Creation-Of-Space"* (*PC-5*) and other similar exercises.

Aside from *"other-determined ejections,"* there is not a lot to *process* for *considerations* on the *"getting out"* part. The *Seeker* already desires to *"be out."* That's the natural state and not the point of *fragmentation*. As we know from *incident-running*: we can't *defragment* *"As-It-Is"* without treating the actual "start" of an *incident*, or finding the earlier "beginning" if necessary. In this case: the earlier beginning of *"being in"* is *"going in."* If one *considers* themselves *"in"* something, they had to *"get in"* in the first place. If an individual is *ejected* at "death," than the *"go in"* would occur at "birth," &tc. We often emphasize the *"Heaven Implanting-Incident"* because it is the undercut to *advanced processing*, being the *entry-point* to the entire *Game* of *this Universe*.

The final part of a *Seeker's* preliminary work for *Wizard Level-1* is *defragmenting* *"ejection"* and *"snap-in" mechanisms* that may be *imprinted* and/or *automatic*. Otherwise, a *Seeker* is likely to experience additional "push–pull" tension between *Self* and the *Body*. Those that have dealt with this phenomenon often describe it rather like the old children's toy of "a ball attached to a paddle with an elastic string." Knowing this, it is better to take steps to prevent it from occurring, rather than having to *"remedy and repair"* it afterward.

The basic *process* for handling *fragmentation* on *"going in"* is given in *PC Lesson-10* (*"Lifting The Veils"*)—in the section titled: *"Metaspiritual Systemology."* It was also used in some procedures for handling *en-*

tities (*AT#5*). While this previously may have been treated lightly, it becomes more critical to handle for *Level-8*.

As an addition to the instructions/background given (in *PC-10*), if a *Seeker* has access to *Biofeedback-Tech*, the advanced practice for this is to check for *fragmented charge* using a *GSR-Meter*. It will *register* on various *command-wording* (or *"hot buttons"*) associated with *"going in,"* if there is *imprinting*. This is then handled with the *Analytical Recall* technique given there, until no more *charge registers* when that *wording* is *"called"* or *"spotted"* or *"run"* during the *process*. [Use only *circuits* "1," "2" and "3"; then use "0" on your second pass through *Wizard Level-1* material.]

For convenience, the standard list of *keywords/buttons* is: *"Go In"*; *"Put In"*; *"Want To Go In"*; *"Must Get In"*; *"Can't Get In"*; *"Kicked Out"*; *"Be Trapped"*; *"Forced In"*; *"Pulled In"* and *"Pushed In."*

[*New Update (for 2024)*: As a result of *systematic processing* being in the public hands for several years—in addition to the widespread distribution of other *"New Age"* practices—it has recently been discovered that a *Seeker* may also need to *process-out* those *incidents* where they: *"Tried To Eject, But Didn't/Couldn't."*]

ADVANCED ABILITY TRAINING ROUTE (*Wizard Level-1 Procedure*)

Advanced Ability Training (AAT) is not *"ejection processing"*—such a procedure does not exist in *Systemology*. These exercises are not intended to *"induce" ejection*; but *ejection* may take place while practicing them. It is true that an ability to handle and direct *ejection* is an intended *end-point* or *end-realization* of this *Wizard-Level*; but it is not what is *processed directly*. [The same AAT route is followed even *after* a *Seeker "ejects."*]

Completing this routine in one single *session* is not required or expected. The *"standard opening procedures"* of a *Formal Session* are not used in *Wizard-Level Training Routines*. At the beginning of each *session*, a *Seeker* must *run* "Preventative Fundamentals" (*PC-9*) as their first *procedure*. This means: checking for *breaks* or *upsets* of *"Flow Factors"* (*PC-7*); making sure *presence* is not on some *problem* elsewhere (*PC-4*); and scanning over any *Harmful-Acts* or *Hold-Backs* that may have our *attention* because *"someone almost found out,"* &tc. (*PC-6*).

When a *Seeker* completes this route/routine, they proceed to the *next* section: "Wizard Level-1 Stabilization." If you find difficulties processing this routine (that are not a result of *entities*, short-cutting previous *processing-levels*, or failing to provide *presence in-session*, &tc.), go directly to *"Wizard Level-1 Stabilization."* It may be used to: *stabilize* results from *Wiz-*

ard Level-1 and/or *enable* one to get better results (if necessary).

Wizard Level-1 puts emphasis on getting a *Seeker willing* and *able* to *knowingly eject Awareness* from its *fixation* on the *Body*. *Wizard Level-2* puts emphasis on increasing the *Spiritual Perception* of a *Seeker* once *ejected*. There is, however, no real distinction between the "type" of *systematic techniques* and exercises used for these purposes. They were all originally researched and experimented with during the same phase of work at the *Systemology Society* (2020–2022). They are all collected and codified in this manual for the first time.

Ejection could occur at any point of any exercise (from either *Wizard-Level*); and any of the exercises (from either *Wizard-Level*) may also be used after *ejection* to improve its *stability*, or even increase *perception*. Some of the techniques appeared in previous lessons. A *Seeker* was often instructed to simply *"imagine"* or accept whatever *"vague perception"* they had on them—or an *"advanced version"* may have been listed as optional. At *Level-8*, we are interested in taking up these earlier suggestions and actually improving *Spiritual Ability*.

Training Routines are *systematic* arrangements of various *processes* and *exercises*. Unlike the work done for *Level-7*, or involving *Implant-Platforms*, this *route* is not mimicking or replicating some specific *incident* or *sequence*. There is no real concern about seeing instructions "out of order" or following a different order.

A. DEFRAG-BY-ATTENTION

In this first step, we want to increase a *Seeker's ability* to *"Defrag-by-Attention."* This step also helps protect against so easily being the effect of future *Implants*. *"The Jewel of Knowledge"* (*AT#3*) is used for this step. A *Seeker* already *processed-out*

"*The Jewel (Part #1-5)*" as an *incident* (for themselves) during *Level-7*.

The goal of this step is to be able to *intentionally* and *knowingly* Create (*Imagine*) and then *Un-Create* (*disperse*) each *item-line* of "*The Jewel.*" A *Seeker* should focus on *copying* the intensity and sensation of the original (*incident*) item, but *not* as a "*recall action.*" [When using *Biofeedback*, if enough significance is put on the *creation*, it will *register* as "*mass.*" This is then *dispersed* ("*defragged-by-attention*") and will cease to *register.*]

A *Seeker* continues this until they feel comfortable doing it easily. They should find it interesting and fun; then be able to see the utter ridiculousness of the *Implant*; then be able to *Create* and *Defrag* any of the *items* from the *Implant* again— *knowingly at will.*

One challenge of *Ascension beyond this Universe*, is that even an *Actualized Seeker* (*Alpha-Spirit*) is likely to hit "*The Jewel*" of *this Universe* and end up right back here (if they have not built up an *"immunity"* to it). Most less-*Aware* individuals do not even make it that far in their *"between-lives period,"* often getting *"caught"* (as *Alpha-Spirits*) by various *"screens"* or *"Implant-Stations"* (*Heaven Implants, &tc.*) before ending up back here.

This is possible because, while the *Alpha-Spirit* is not *actually located* within *this Physical Universe*, its *fixed Awareness* and *considerations-of-Beingness* very much are —even after they are *released* from a *Body*, whether through *body-death,* or intentional *ejection-of-Awareness*.

Ejecting from the *Body* alone does not put one *"outside"* or *"exterior to"* the *Physical Universe*. There are other *postulates, reality-agreements, considerations, entities,* and *fragments*, that also contribute to a confinement to, or *fixation* with, *this Universe*—and which require *total defragmentation* to *master Ascension*.

B. SOURCE-OF-SENSATION

This step is to get *certainty* on *ability* to *create sensation* independent of a *body-perception*.

"Create (Imagine) 'Heat' Until The Body
  Seems Warmer."

C. SOURCE-OF-LIGHT

This step is to get *certainty* on *ability* to *create* a *light-source* independent of *this Physical Universe*. It is *not* necessary for this *light* to be objectively visible or manifest (perceivable to others) in *this Physical Universe.* Alternate: *Creating (Imagining)* and *Un-Creating (dispersing)* a *light-source.* [This *light-source* should not be *"electrical"* (a light-bulb) or *"nuclear"* (like a sun).]

D. SOURCE-OF-BODY-ACTION

Alternate:

1. "Move The Body."
2. "Realize Who Is Making It Move."

E. UNDERSCORE{UNIVERSE FUNDAMENTALS}

Run the *"Preventative Fundamentals"* (PC-9, *&tc.*) on each of the following (separately):

SPACE; TIME; ENERGY; and MATTER.

F. SPOTTING-THIS-UNIVERSE

Run *"Orientation in Space-Time"* (PC-1) outside (in a public place): *"Spotting"* (*looking* at something and *noticing* something about it) each of the following (separately):

SPACE; TIME; ENERGY; MATTER; AN OBJECT; AN ANIMAL; A PERSON; SELF; THE UNIVERSE; ANOTHER'S PERSONAL UNIVERSE; WHAT YOU ARE DOING NOW; WHAT ANOTHER IS DOING NOW.

G. SPOTTING POINTS-IN-SPACE

This step is practiced comfortably lying down; eyes closed. Alternate:

1. *"Spot One Point In The Room."*

2. *"Spot One Point In The Body."*

When a *Seeker* is comfortable with this (and *perception* of it is no longer *changing, improving, &tc.*), then continue this step using *"Two Points.."*; and finally *"Three Points.."* [Versions of this were introduced in *PC-10* and *PC-12*.]

When a *Seeker* can do this step easily, follow this same progressive procedure; but alternating: *"...Point(s) In The Room"* and *"...Point(s) Outside."* [If necessary, the second part may be clarified as *"...Outside The Room (or Building)."*]

H. CREATING AN ILLUSION

This step is practiced comfortably lying down; eyes closed. Alternate:

1. *"Create (Imagine)."*

2. *"Intend."*

In the first part: a *Seeker Creates/Imagines* "something" (an *object*, an *energy*, a *condition*, an *illusion*, &tc.).

The second part is repeated many times, *Intending* various things about the *creation*. The suggested list of *intentions* (for PCL) are: *"Hold It Still"*; *"Conserve It"*; *"Protect It"*; *"Control It"*; *"Keep It From Going Away"*; *"Hide It"*; *"Change It"*; *"Rearrange It"*; *"Duplicate It"* (in its same space); *"Turn It Upside-Down"*; *"Turn It On Its Side"*; *"Move It"* (and *"Move It Back"*); *"Be It"*; *"Not-Be It"*; *"Destroy It"*; *"Create It" (Again)* and *"Destroy It"* at will.

I. SPOTTING DISTANCES

This step is usually practiced outside. Alternate:

1. *"Spot (Put Attention On) An Object."*

2. *"Notice The Distance (Space) Between You And It."*

J. PROJECTING ENERGY-BEAMS

This step is usually practiced with a combination of *intention* and *visualization*.

This is done outside and/or inside. Note any *realizations*. [Handling *"spiritual energy"* is introduced at *Processing Level-6 (PC-13)*.]

1. *"Spot (Put Attention On) An Object."*

2. *"Place (Put Out) An Energy Beam, Wrapped Around You And It."*

3. *"Pull Yourself Toward It By Shortening (Retracting) The Beam."*

K. RECEIVING (DRAWING) ENERGY

This step is usually practiced with a combination of *intention* and *visualization*. This is done outside and/or inside. Repeat it a dozen times. Note any *realizations*.

1. *"Spot (Put Attention On) An Object."*

2. *"Draw Energy (Out) From It And Into You."*

When a *Seeker* has done this step comfortably on a few objects: practice STEP-I, STEP-J, and STEP-K, on "A CLOUD."

L. <u>LEVEL-7 A.T. STABILIZATION</u>

"The Jewel of Knowledge" (*AT#3*) is used for this step. Refer to the section: *"Level-7 Stabilization Point."* Complete the steps as given for that procedure (outdoors).

Then practice the procedure indoors; eyes closed. You can *Imagine* (*get a sense*) or use *ZU-Vision* (if possible) to: *"Look Around A City And Spot.."* [Practice it *"mentally/spiritually"*; but not as a *"recall"* of being outdoors.]

When this step is completed, a *Seeker* continues to the next section.

WIZARD LEVEL-1 STABILIZATION

The following exercises are derived from the original *Systemology Wizard Training Regimen*—many of which were introduced in the *"Pathway"* *Professional Course (PC)*. For this *stabilization proced-*

ure, a *Seeker* uses the *"advanced version"* (if applicable) of any *processes*. [Apply *"standard opening procedures"* (*Formal Session*) to these *sessions*. Refer to original materials (where indicated) for any additional background or instruction.]

A. <u>TOUCH-AND-LET-GO</u> (*PC-1*)

This step is practiced lying down; eyes closed. Use *advanced version* on:

1. Objects in the room.
2. Specific "spots" in the room.
3. Objects outside (the room).
4. "Spots" outside (the room).

["*Spots*" means "*Spots-in-Space*"—or a small focused area of *Space*—not otherwise defined, or occupied, by *Mass*. A *Seeker* may initially practice using "*specific spots on a (blank) wall*" for "*spots in the room.*"]

B. <u>"THE WALL"</u> (*PC-1*)

This step is practiced lying down; *body's*

69

eyes closed. Use *advanced version* to: "*look*" at the *Wall*; "*touch*" the *Wall*; and "*turn around.*" [This is a popular *process* among *Seekers*, often *run* until an actual *ejection* (*Spiritual Perception*) occurs; but that is not its original purpose.]

C. EMOTIONAL FLOWS (*PC-2*)

This step has two parts, each is *run* on various "neutral" *objects* present; then a *Wall*; then with eyes closed (using something the *Seeker* has *Created/Imagined*). This is done by *intention*. But a *Seeker* should continue this until they get a real *sense* of it happening. The following is only an outline. [Use the instructions in *PC-2.*]

1a. Spot an Object/Wall/Creation.

1b. "Feel" various emotions about it.

2a. Spot an Object/Wall/Creation.

2b. Make it "feel" various emotions about you.

D. <u>COMMUNICATION</u> (*PC-3*)

Practice this step of *communication* with an *object*; then a *Wall*; then *parts* of the *Body*. Use *intention* and/or *Imagine* the *communication-and-acknowledgment* cycles —"*Hello,*" "*Thank You,*" &tc.
[Refer to *PC-3*.]

E. <u>"BELL, BOOK & CANDLE"</u> (*PC-3*)

This step is practiced lying down; eyes closed. Use *advanced version*.
[Refer to *PC-3*.]

F. <u>CREATIVENESS PROCESSING</u> (*PC-5*)

This step is practiced with eyes closed. It requires a *Seeker* to be able to *Create/Imagine* and actually *see* or *get a sense* that their *creations* are there. It is sometimes necessary to "*create*" and "*throw away*" a few before one is satisfied with their level of *perception* (or *perfection* of the *creation*).

A *godlike being* should be able to "*create,*" "*destroy*" and "*re-create*" *anything*. While operating at *this* level of existence, our best route of exercising this *creative ability* is *"mentally"* or *"imaginatively."* In *PC-5,* the suggestion is for *"acceptance," "rejection"* and *"substitutions"* for anything (like "money" or "pain"). In essence, a *Seeker* increases their tolerance to *"take it"* or *"leave it."* It is also useful in *processing,* to *"invent ways to waste it."* [*Update*: also process-out *"accepting it under duress"* or *"forced to have it."*]

There is no standard *terminal item-list* of suggested *objects* or *creations* given here. Typically, worksheets and data from earlier *sessions* are used to determine if *residual fragmentation* remains on anything specific. A list could be developed by scanning *terminals* and *concepts* that represent each *Sphere of Existence* (and even the *Arcs of Infinity*). The only challenge here with *Solo-Processing,* is that a *Solo-Pilot* is more likely to *avoid* areas and *terminals* that they *"don't like"* (which defeats the purpose of the exercise).

G. <u>PLACES YOU ARE NOT</u> (*PC-6*)

This step (with eyes open or closed) operates by having a *Seeker* put *attention* on
"*exterior*" (or *remote from the body*) *locations* to "check" to see that they "are not
there." *Spot* many places. [This is another
popular *process* that *Seekers* often *run* until
an actual *ejection* occurs.]

"*Spot Places You Are Not.*"

H. <u>HANDLING ORDERS</u> (*PC-7*)

This step is based on the "*advanced
processing*" section in *PC-7*. Cycle through
these PCL on one *terminal*, getting as
many answers as you can, before going to
the next one.

The *terminals* are: PEOPLE; THINGS;
   PLACES; GROUPS; GOVERNMENTS;
   LIFEFORMS; ENERGIES; and SPIRITS.

  1. "*Spot Some ___ You Are Not Giving
     Orders To.*"

  2. "*Spot Some ___ That Are Not Giving
     You Orders.*"

3. *"Spot Some ___ That Are Not Giving Orders To Others."*

4. *"Spot Some ___ That Are Not Receiving Orders From Others."*

5. *"Spot Some ___ That Are Not Giving Orders To Themselves."*

After completing the above to a satisfactory end-point, a *Seeker* takes up the other side of this with the PCL below; for when they *agreed to follow another's orders* for the sake of *having a game*. [Refer to *PC-12* and *AT#2* for what we mean by *"game."*] Rehabilitation of "handling orders" means a *total freedom* of *choice* about *following* or *disagreeing* with "orders" — *not compulsively* one way or the other.

1. *"Spot An Incident When You Chose To Follow Another's Orders (for the sake of having a game)."*

2. *"Notice Some Things About It."*

Then *Spot* an *earlier incident*, and so on, until you reach the *earliest* one accessible; and *run* that. [The *upper-level* handling of any *turbulence* that does not immediately *disperse-on-realization* (*defrag-by-attention*) is to alternate: "*Spot Something In The Incident; Spot Something In The Room (Environment).*"]

1. "*Spot An Incident Where You Convinced Others To Follow Your Orders (for the sake of having a game).*"

2. "*Notice Some Things About It.*"

Handle *earlier/earliest* as above.

Then practice the other *advanced exercises* for "*Attacking,*" "*Hate,*" "*Beauty*" and "*Safe To Be*" as given in *PC-7*.

I. (NOT)-KNOWINGNESS (*PC-10*)

Perform this step exactly as given in *PC-10*.

J. ADVANCED EXERCISES (*PC-10*)

Perform this step by completing all *ten* bullet-pointed {"•"} exercises given in the final section of *PC-10*. They are summarized as follows:

1. *Create/Imagine copies* of your (current) *Body*.

2. *Create/Imagine* "ideal" or "healthy" *copies* of your *Body*.

3. *Looking* into a mirror: *something there; nothing there*.

4. "Mentally" (or in *ZU-Vision*) decide *To Be* (as a *viewpoint*) in a *public place*; notice *scenery* and *motion*.

5. Using *Step-4: Create/Imagine* and *Uncreate* (*disperse*) *copies* of your *Body being* there *in front* of your *viewpoint*.

6. Using *Step-5*: alternate *viewpoints*; "inside" and "outside" the *Body*.

7. Using *Step-6*: get a sense of others acknowledging the *Body being* there.

8. Using a *"basic solid shape"* to represent the *Body* for previous exercises.

9. Moving the *"basic solid shape"* around like a playing piece.

10. Performing the exercises using different *Body-Types*.

K. <u>COLLAPSED-SPACE PROCESSING</u>

The *"collapse-of-space"* phenomenon—having *Space* *"collapse-in"* on one—is *processed* similarly to the *"getting-in"* or *"going-inside"* *fragmentation* (given in earlier material) that we apply to all *Seekers* (including *entities*). [This *process* should be *added* to all *entity-handling procedures.*]

As with processing *"getting-in,"* this step is also *run* using a list of *keywords/buttons*. In this case, we are treating an even "higher magnitude" of *incident*. In fact, its original development concerned *processing-out* the *loss* of *"Home Universe"* and subsequent *fragmentation* concerning "world-closed-in" type of *incidents.*

Recall data from that far on the *Backtrack* may not be readily accessible to a *Seeker,* so they should do the best they can—and an individual has likely experienced many other *space-collapsing incidents* since then. It is important not to "push" too hard on vivid *recall,* or you may end up "pulling" in *imprinting* from an *entity* that is in close proximity—and misidentifying the *imprint* as your own (and it will persist in restimulation).

The *fragmented charge* on the *keywords* is best determined with *Meter-reads*. The *charge* is *dispersed* by *running "Recall"* on that *item* (using all *circuits*) and *dispersing-by-realization* or *Spotting* (until it no longer *registers* on the *GSR-Meter*). The list of *keywords/buttons* for this new process are:

1. *World Closed In*

2. *Space Collapsed*

3. *(Your) Energy Collapsed*

4. *Anchor (or Dimension) Points Collapsed*

5. *Anchor (Dimension) Points Snapped-In*

6. *Everything Fell In (and/or Down)*

7. *Space Was Uncreated (or Dispersed or Un-Space)*

8. *(Your) Energy Was Uncreated (or Dispersed)*

9. *(Your) Frame Of Reference Collapsed*

10. *Caved-In*

11. *Pulled Back*

12. *Withdrew From Everything*

13. *Made It All Unreal*

When this *stabilization point* is completed, a *Seeker* may then return to the top of *Wizard Level-1 Procedure*, if desired (or still left incomplete). If "*entities*" or other *somatic-pings* have become intrusive to personal development, or it seems some "*blockage*" has become active as a result of *Wizard Training*, then a handling of "*entities*" (*&tc.*) may be required.

However, a *Seeker* should not become so immersed in, or enamored by the idea of, treating "*entities*" that there is no *session-time* available for their own *Wizard Training*. There is sometimes a point where you just need to strongly *intend* a *mass-communication* (*to them all*) that *"everyone will get processed in their own turn."*

Ideally, a *Seeker* will continue onto (and complete) *Wizard Level-2 Procedure* before treating the material of *"Entities & Fragments"* (*AT#5*) a second time.

Having *"spiritual perception"* is not the determinant factor of *Wizard Level-1* completion; only one's own *certainty* that they have *ejected Awareness "exterior to"* the *Body* is necessary. No matter what one's skill-level or experience, the next set of exercises given for *Wizard Level-2* can enhance the *certainty* that is now there—and the *perception* will follow.

EJECTION, PERCEPTION & BARRIERS
(*Wizard Level-2 Keynote Lecture*)

In *Systemology*, we are frequently concerned with *viewpoints*—which is to say *"a point from which to view," "point-of-*

view" or "POV." In the first two *Wiz-ard-Levels*, the emphasis is specifically on, what are often called, *"remote view-points"*—because they are at *"points"* the *Alpha-Spirit* is *"viewing"* (or *perceiving*) from that are *"remote"* (or *"exterior-to"*) the *sensory-perception* and *viewpoints* of a located *Body* (or *genetic vehicle*).

Ejection-of-Awareness is really a matter of one's *considerations* and *certainty* far more than any specific procedure. The same may be said concerning improvement of *Spiritual Perception*. True progress on the *Pathway* is marked by a *Seeker's* increasing ability to actually *change their considera-tions*—or *"change their minds,"* so to speak. Many individuals are under the delusion that they already maintain this total freedom.

To handle *Spiritual Perception*, a *Wizard* would have to be able to handle *Energy* and *Space*, and of course, *Force*. An indi-vidual doesn't do this when operating within the *Human Condition.* There are all kinds of *sensors* and *filters* and *communication relays*—all kinds of various *machinery*—that are in the way of *actually* "seeing" this Universe. When a *Seeker* first "ejects," they are not really expected to have very vivid *perception.*

When we operate within the confines of the *Human Condition*—or more accurately, a *fixed viewpoint* within a *Body*—we are *perceiving* (or *receiving* "signals" and "cues" from) a *Universe* that is really only "energy-waves," "standing-waves of mass," "particles," and various "forces." All of this is transmitted and translated by all kinds of *mechanisms* and *machinery* before the *Mind-System* "projects" it on a kind of "screen" for the *Alpha-Spirit* to "view" and *perceive* as its own experience. Therefore, an individual is not really in the habit of *perceiving directly.*

Anything that hinders *perception* would be best defined as a *"barrier"*—*"barriers to perception*." Perhaps one of the more fundamental issues is just how many "*barriers*" an individual is *fixated on perceiving*—or is *compulsively* (or *unknowingly*) "*looking through*" in order *to perceive*.

A preoccupation with *barriers* generally defines our "*thoughts*" or "*thinkingness*." When we compare the state of *Knowingness* to levels of *Thinkingness*, all our "thinking" serves to do is handle *barriers*—either avoiding or overcoming them in some way. To be so preoccupied with them, is of course, to be at an *agreement-level* with them, and even at an *effect-level* that is below their mechanics or structure.

The experience of *this Physical Universe* via the *Human Condition* is considered the section of the "*Beta-Awareness Scale*" that falls between *zero* and *four* on our *Standard Model*. The *Human Condition* being: *Alpha-Spirit* plus a *genetic-vehicle*. But the *Standard Model* extends well beyond the

Human Condition—it extends from *Infinity* to *Infinity*, and to that which we classify as *Alpha-Awareness* or *Actualized Awareness*.

While our *Standard Model does* systematize upper-level *Actualized Alpha* existence above *"four,"* there is also the *low-Awareness* scale that an *Alpha-Spirit* can maintain independent of a *Body*, that extends "out the bottom" *below zero* and *Body Death*. It consists of remorse for a *Body*; the need to protect a *Body*; even not wanting anything to do with a *Body*; but still very much *fixated* on *"bodies."*

When an individual *"ejects"* from a *Body*, by one means or another, there is no guarantee they are going "out the top" of the *Beta-Awareness Scale*; in fact, when individuals return to the *Human Condition* in their next "lifetime" or "incarnation" (after *Body Death*), it would suggest that they do not *"ascend out the top"* automatically (or by default).

84

Another *sub-zero Awareness-level* is: the use of *bodies* for *hiding in*. The *sensory-functions* of a *Body* allow it to be used by an *Alpha-Spirit* as a personal buffer for handling and *perceiving* the *energy* and *force* of *this Universe*. Over the course of our *fragmented* experience of many *Universes*, we have gotten a bit wise to the fact that these *energy-waves* and *force-fields* are able to be used against us (because we have *considered* such for this *level* of *reality-agreements*) and so we are reluctant to start *confronting* or handling them directly.

As the primary *barrier* an individual has to *getting-out* of their *Body*, or a *Head*, is their own *fixed ideas*: it stands to reason that a *Seeker* may be carrying a lot of *fear* —or some sense of *danger* or *mystery*— concerning what might be "*out there*"; or what they *fear* they might have to handle as a *Spiritual Being* that is free from the *Human Condition*. The result is a *Spiritual*

Being that has become *compulsively dependent* on *bodies* — and this *Physical Universe* — for "orientation-points" or "anchor-points" to experience its own *Beingness.*

Space is also *perceived* as a *barrier* to *Knowingness.* Although it seems like an "invisible barrier," the layered effect that we perceive at a great *distance* from *Earth* gives us the sense that it is *layers* of *darkness, blackness, unknowingness,* and *mystery.* This better explains our theory behind one of the *Wizard-Level* exercises, where a *Seeker* "imagines" many concentric spheres within spheres — or *layers* — of *darkness* or *blackness,* and then practices "looking through" these spheres or *layers.* Understanding the basic theory of this *keynote lecture* will help a *Seeker* understand the purpose behind practicing the exercises provided for *Wizard-Levels 1* and 2.

R.S.V.P—REMOTE SPIRITUAL VIEWPOINTS & PERCEPTION
(*Wizard Level-2 Procedure*)

Wizard Level-2 Procedure is approached similarly to *Wizard Level-1*. In this case, however, there is no change in *routine* if a *Seeker* finds difficulty with the steps. The remedy is simply to start from the top and work through those exercises for which one *does* have *certainty* on before attempting more difficult steps again. This should not be interpreted as a *loss*, because a *Seeker* will likely work through *Wizard Level-2 Procedure* multiple times to increase their handling of *ejection* and *perception.*

Completing this routine in one single *session* is not required or expected. The "*standard opening procedures*" of a *Formal Session* are not used in *Wizard-Level Training Routines*. Instead, at the beginning of each *session,* a *Seeker runs* "*Preventative Fundamentals*" (*PC-9*) as their first *process* (as they did with *Wizard Level-1*). A *Seeker* may also find that using some kind of "*blindfold*" is helpful when practicing some exercises.

A. EJECTION-OF-AWARENESS

At some point during the *Wizard-Level* work, a *Seeker* is likely to come across their preferred or favored *process(es)* or method(s) to "induce" or "assist" *ejection.* This is something that can only be determined after applying the various exercises suggested throughout this manual.

Wizard Level-2 is designed for a *Seeker* that has already achieved an *ejection-of-Awareness*; and is used to further develop that as a "*conscious ability.*" Although some exercises are more commonly used than others for "*ejection,*" a direct method is not something we can specifically instruct for STEP-A.

"The Wall," "Places You Are Not," "Back Upper Corner-Points Of The Room," "3 Points In Body; 3 Points In Room," and *"3 Points In Room; 3 Points Outside Of This Universe"* are all popularly used (and some even directly appear in this *routine*). But, this does not rule out the potential for a *Seeker* to make a basic high-power *Intention* (*a Self-made command*) for simply "stepping out" (*ejecting*) at will.

The first time *ejection* is directly implied on the *Pathway*, is in the final exercise of *PC-10*—which is the final lesson of *Processing Level-4* and basic *Beta-Defragmentation Procedure*. [*Processing-Levels 5 & 6 are Pre-A.T. levels*.] In *PC-10* it describes it as: "...the ability to *conceive of* or *maintain a sense of* "centering" and "focusing" your own *Awareness* as a *viewpoint* (POV) a few feet *behind* the *head* of your current *Body*."

After *ejection*—before a *Seeker* is directed to do anything or go anywhere or look at the *Body*—the first several steps of this *routine* are intended to *stabilize* the *ejected-*state.

B. <u>MAKING COPIES</u> (*PC-2/PC-12*)

The basic PCL for this step are:

1. *"What Are You Looking At?"*
2. *"Make A Copy. (Make Many Copies)."*

With the *body's eyes* closed, post-*ejection*: the *Seeker* *"makes"* (*Creates/Imagines*) copies of whatever they are looking at—whatever they see. No matter what it is—however vague or fuzzy—you just *copy* what is there over and over again.

After you have several copies, you *"push them all together."* The first batch you *"pull the copies in on yourself"*; then the next batch of copies you can *"throw away"* (and continue alternating in this wise). This helps to remedy the *"loss of mass"* feeling after *ejecting* from the *Body*.

[Only *"pull in on yourself"* if you have *knowingly ejected* and are *"exterior to"* a *Body*. Otherwise, as a purely *imaginative exercise*, you would *"push them in on the Body."* Never *"pull-in"* while your *view-point* is from *inside the Body.* Get a sense of *"pushing-in"* from the *outside.* This step can be repeated throughout the routine to remedy whenever a *Seeker* feels their "attention thinning" from excessive exercises while *ejected.*]

The *vividness* of *perception*, or the *scenery* altogether, may change several times after treating the *copies.* You just keep *copying* whatever presents itself until there is no longer a change of perception (*e.g.*, vividness or detail isn't improving; scenery isn't shifting around). Then we balance the *somethingness* with the *Nothingness.* A *Seeker* extends or reaches their *Awareness* to *"Spot a Nothingness"* and then *copies* that for a while before going to STEP-C.

C. REACHING & HOLDING

Variations of this exercise appear in

"opening procedures" of a *Formal Session*; and in *"Creation-Of-Space"* processes (*PC-5*). *Locating,* and *holding attention on,* *"corner-points"* of a square room is a form of *"Creation-Of-Space"* (defining "boundaries" or *dimension-points* of perceived *Space*).

Usually only two *corner-points* are used for this exercise—and they are often the "upper-back" *corner-points* of a room (or whatever is *behind* the *Body*), which forces *attention-Awareness* to *reach* in a direction other than what is in front of the *Seeker*.

This exercise can be modified to begin with *one corner-point*; and be extended to use all *four upper-corners* of a room—or even all *eight corner-points* (that form a "cube").

[*Update*: a *Seeker* should always end this exercise by *"letting go"* of any *corner-points* being *"held."*]

D. <u>PLACES YOU ARE NOT</u> (*PC-6*)

This step includes a *process* repeated from *Wizard Level-1*. A *Seeker* puts *attention* on "*remote locations*" to "check" to see that they "are not there."

  "*Spot A Place You Are Not. (Spot Many Places)*."

[*Update*: in *Traditional Piloting*, an effective transition from the previous step is: "*Now, Let Go; and Spot Some Places You Are Not.*"]

To effectively practice this step: a *Seeker* doesn't just quickly rattle off a list of arbitrary places. The goal is to actually *look* and *have certainty* from a particular *viewpoint* of *Space*.

E. <u>ABILITY-TO-CONFRONT</u>

This step asks a *Seeker* to *Spot* "things" (with the *body's eyes* closed) that they *consider* comfortable (or "safe") to *look at* (*confront*). This could also apply to "emotions" (or people displaying emotions).

This is meant to increase tolerance for handling the *Physical Universe.*

This is not a *creativeness process.* A *Seeker* is not intended to *Create/Imagine* "things" to *look at*—but to actually "go" and *view* them in *this Physical Universe.* The accuracy of the *perception* is not as important as the actual *intention* to "be" at various *viewpoints.*

The basic PCL for this step are:

1. *"Spot Something It Would Be Safe To Look At In This Room."*

2. *"Spot Something It Would Be Safe To Look At Outside This Room."*

F. SHARED-SPACE

Part of the *reality-agreements* and *Implanted-Postulates* for *this Universe* include the *consideration* that *"two things* can't occupy the same *Space."* So long as a *Seeker* has heavy charge on this *consideration*—and the *consideration* that they, themselves, occupy a *Body* with *mass*—much of what an *Alpha-Spirit* is capable of would *seem* like a logical impossibility.

"*What wouldn't you mind sharing the same space with?*"

–or–

"*What wouldn't you mind sharing the same space with you?*"

Not *actually* having a *mass* present in *this Universe*, the *Alpha-Spirit* is very much capable of utilizing a *viewpoint* that does share *Space* with something that has *mass*. This step increases *Awareness* (and tolerance) on *ability* to *change* one's *Beingness*. The *process* is *run* to an *end-realization*, or all answers are exhausted.

G. <u>LOCATIONAL VIEWPOINTS</u> (*PC-5*)

This is based on a *meditation* found in "*eastern spiritual traditions.*" A version, treated as an *imaginative exercise*, appears in *PC-5* (and should be reviewed for additional instruction and background).

[In *Traditional Piloting*, a *Co-Pilot* delivers *"locational"* PCL as quickly as a *Seeker* can perform them. This is generally determined by the observed *communication-lag* in responses.]

The PCL-sequence given in *PC-5* is:

1. *"Be Near (or Above) ___."*

2a. *"Be Inside Of ___."*

2b. *"Be Outside Of ___."*

3a. *"Be At The Center Of ___."*

3b. *"Be Outside Of ___."*

4a. *"Be On The Surface Of ___."*

4b. *"Be Above ___."*

[Note that the PCL-*keyword* (*trigger* or *button*) for POV-*Locational* (type) *A.T. processing* is "BE" (not "MOVE TO"). "Motion" between perceived *distances* in *space-time* is not a *consideration* (or *factor*) of the action.]

The applications for this exercise are unlimited. The original technique is called *"journeying to other planets"* —hence the *terminals* that a *Seeker* finds most interesting/effective for this *process* are "*planets.*"

A *systematic* approach would begin with being "*near the Earth*" or "*in the Sky*" before departing for other *planets*. Other preferred *terminals* are "*The Moon,*" "*The Sun,*" and "*Mars.*" It is best to *run* a few cycles of being "*near*" each of these *target-terminals* (with the first PCL) before *adding* the next PCL-set (*inside/outside, &tc.*) to the cycle.

A variation of this "*change-of-space*" technique is often used in *defragmentation processing*. By alternating the *direction* of *attention*, a *Seeker* is really "*shifting,*" between (for example) "*Being In The Incident*" and "*Being In The Room,*" *&tc.* This gives a *Seeker* certainty that what they're "holding onto" is really "somewhere else."

A *Seeker* already has too many *Universes* confused with, or superimposed over, *their own*. One purpose of *A.T.* exercises is for a *Seeker* to *get a sense* of *"separateness"* —*not "connectedness"*—with *this Physical Universe.*

H. <u>OWNERSHIP-OF-REALITY</u> (*PC-11*)

With the *body's eyes* open: *select* a certain section of *"wall"*—like a circular *spot* that is a few feet in diameter. This can also be done with large (significant, heavy, *&tc.*) objects that are in view. Alternate (repeatedly):

1. *"Get The Idea That You Are Creating It."*

2. *"Get The Idea That ___ Is Creating It."*

For the second PCL, use each of the following terminals separately (*running* each to a satisfactory *end-point* before going to the next):

ANOTHER; SOCIETY; LIFEFORMS; A BODY; (YOUR) {SPIRITUAL} MACHINERY; THE {OBJECT ITSELF}; THE PHYSICAL UNIVERSE; AGREED-UPON MACHINERY; SPIRITS; and (A) GOD.

A *Seeker* may discover that *they* (*them-*

98

selves) are *not* the one *creating* everything —although it is in their capability. Most of the time, it will be discovered that "old machinery" is responsible for things persisting.

I. <u>BODY-SYMPATHY</u>

When the *Body* is severely *injured*, or even *dies*, an individual that is *fixedly* "*interior*" will *eject* suddenly—but then quickly "*snap-in*" again. This is because when "*exterior to*" a *Body*, at *low-Awareness* levels, an *Alpha-Spirit* has a *reactive-tendency* to "sympathize" with a *Body*. It "*snaps-in*" to try and "protect" or "heal" or even "reanimate" it.

This *process* is included here because it assists in overcoming the general impulse and tendency, while demonstrating both *interiorizing* and *ejection*. This can be *run* as "*imaginatively*" (or as "*actually*") as one's current *ability/perception* allows for. [The *end-realization* is that actions to "*fix*"

(*&tc.*) something are best handled *from* the *"outside."*]

1. *"Look Around The Room And Choose An Object. (Preferably large)."*

2. *"Decide That There Is Something Wrong With It. (Pretend anything)."*

3. *"Feel Sorry For The Object; Sympathize With It; Say, 'Oh, Poor Thing'."*

4a. *"Imagine Yourself 'Going-In-To' The Object To 'Fix It'."*

4b. *"Decide That You Are 'Inside' The Object; Its Mass Is All Around You."*

5a. *"Look Around 'Inside' The Object."*

5b. *"Realize That 'Inside' Is Not A Good Place To 'Fix It' From; That You Made A Mistake 'Going-In'."*

6a. *"Eject Awareness From The Object; Imagine That You Are Looking Down At It."*

6b. *"Imagine 'Fixing It' From The 'Outside'; Imagine 'Putting' An 'Energy Beam' On It And Say, 'There,*

That Fixes It'."

7. "Let Go Of It. (Select Another Object And Repeat The Process)."

For your second application (in a separate *session*): *run* the *process* on "Created/Imagined" objects rather than the physical ones (in a room).

For your third application: *run* the *process* on "dead bodies" (*Imagined*). For "6b" alternate: "*fixing it successfully from the outside (to resurrect it)*" and "*deciding it isn't worth the trouble and abandoning it.*"

[This *process* may also be practiced on the *Body*. You can *perceive* "*putting out*" or "*projecting*" *energy beams* on anything; getting the *Universe* to directly respond with a physical *effect* is another matter, and a higher gradient of work.]

J. TRUTH/UNTRUTH

Alternate the following PCL:

1. "Spot 3 Things That Are True."

2. *"Spot 3 Things That Are Not True."*

3. *"Spot 3 Things That Are True For Someone Else."*

4. *"Spot 3 Things That Are Not True For Someone Else."*

5. *"Spot 3 Things That Are True For Others."*

6. *"Spot 3 Things That Are Not True For Others."*

K. THE RIGHT-TO-BE

This step is often practiced outdoors (in public); but as an *"eyes-closed ZU-Vision" process*, it may also be done alone—indoors or in Nature, *&tc.*

This *process* is an *exercise* in *intention*. It is also a practice of *"permitting freedom"* and *"granting livingness"* (which is important for handling *all beings*; not just *"entities"*). Each PCL is done several times (*with full intention*) on several *"target-terminals"* before going to the next; then repeat the full cycle.

[The emphasis of the *process* is found in the first two PCL.]

1. *"Grant Things/People (Another) The Right To Be There."*

2. *"Grant Things/People (Another) The Right To Do What They're Doing."*

3. *"Imagine Things/People (Another) Giving You The Right To Grant Rights."*

4. *"Grant Others The Right To Grant Rights."*

L. <u>NO-BARRIERS</u>

Alternate the PCL:

1. *"Spot Some Barriers That Are Not In Front Of Your Face."*

2. *"Spot Some Barriers That Are Not Behind You."*

3. *"Spot Some Barriers That Are Not On Your Right Side."*

4. *"Spot Some Barriers That Are Not On Your Left Side."*

5. *"Spot Some Barriers That Are Not Above You."*

6. *"Spot Some Barriers That Are Not Below You."*

M. <u>BLACKNESS (AND MYSTERY)</u>

Run the PCL:

1. *"Look Around The Room And Choose An Object."*

2. *"Create/Imagine a Standing-Wave (or Field) Of Blackness In Front Of It."*

3. *"Alternate A Few Times: Fixing Your Attention On The Blackness; And Taking It Off."*

Continue *running* this *process* until you have no "attraction" to the "*Blackness*" (*Veil of Mystery*); and although you have *intended* for it to be there, you can ignore it and "*look through*" it. [*Disperse* the "*standing-wave*" at the end.]

Then repeat the *process* on another object. Then apply the same *process* to *Created/*

Imagined objects. [Certainty on this step is required for the next one.]

N. <u>LAYERS-OF-BLACKNESS</u>

Run the PCL (with eyes closed):

1. *"Create/Imagine Many Layers Of Blackness Around You."*

2. *"Look Through Each Layer (In Turn) To See The Next One."*

O. <u>IN-AND-OUT ON OBJECTS</u>

Run the PCL:

1. *"Look Around The Room And Choose An Object."*

2a. *"Get The Sense Of 'Going-In-To' The Object; And Being It."*

2b. *"Imagine Being The Object, In The Object, As Vividly As You Can."*

3. *"Eject From The Object."*

Repeat several times and on different objects. This may also be practiced with ZU-*Vision*: *Spotting* objects outside the

105

session-room (in a city, *&tc.*) and *"going-in-and-out"* them. [This exercise is found among some of the most ancient mystical practices and *"Hermetic"* training.]

P. EMOTIONAL-INDEPENDENCE

Run the PCL:

1. *"Decide To Feel An Emotion; And Feel It."*

2. *"Make The Body Feel A Different Emotion."*

[You continue *feeling* the original emotion, while the *Body* experiences another.]

Q. CONSIDERATION-OF-BEINGNESS

Run the PCL:

1. *"What Kind Of Object Can You Be For Certain?"*

2. *"Be It; And Experience It."*

Repeat many times. [Then *run* as: *"What Kind of Energy.."* and *"What Kind Of Space.."*]

R. ENERGY-SOURCES

This *process* is applied only after a *Seeker* has handled the ability to identify *"Sources"* and *"What Is"* (*PC-11*) and understands what *"energy"* means (*PC-13/PC-14*).

The basic PCL for this step is:

"*Create (Imagine) An Energy-Source.*"

  –or–

"*Create (Imagine) Something To Give You Energy.*"

Repeat many times with many things. [A *Seeker* can do this with increasing magnitude, beginning with *generators* and *power-stations*, then working up to *sunstars* and *spiritual machinery*. This *process* is *run* to give a *Seeker* certainty that *they* (*themselves*) are their own *energy-source* for *Creating/Imagining* these *mental images*; and also to loosen *considerations* regarding dependency on "external" *energy-sources*.]

S. TERMINALS

Alternate the PCL:

1. *"Spot Two ___ That You Don't Object To Having Together."*

2. *"Spot Two ___ That You Don't Object To Having Apart."*

Repeat many times on each of the following *terminals* (in turn):

PARTICLES; OBJECTS; ANIMALS; PEOPLE; and SPACES.

T. DISAGREEMENT-WITH-GRAVITY

The basic PCL for this step are:

1. *"Get A Sense Of 'Falling Upwards'."*

2. *"Get A Sense Of Other Things 'Falling Upwards'."*

A *Seeker* should stay on one PCL to get a real certainty on their *"sense"* or *"impression"* before alternating.

U. ENERGY AND MACHINERY

Professional Course material for *"Spiritual Energy"* (PC-13) and *"Spiritual Machinery"* (*PC-14*) should be reviewed and all exercises practiced (in their advanced versions, if applicable). Given the progress a *Seeker* has since made, they should have a greater reality on the previous material when revisiting it at *Level-8*.

V. INTERIORIZATION PRACTICE (*PC-5*)

In this step, a *Seeker* practices "going into" (*interiorizing*) and "getting-out of" (*ejecting*) many various *terminals* — objects, animals, people, buildings, mountains, planets, suns, galaxies, universes, &*tc.* (to the extent of their *ability* and *perception*).

W. SPLITTING (VIEWPOINTS)

A *Seeker* "Imagines" their *Awareness-of-Beingness* "splitting" into two: *being* both "*in the Body*" and "*exterior-to it*" simultaneously.

APPENDIX: WIZARD-LEVEL SESSION
(*Basic Script Example*)

0a. *"Start of Session."*
0b. *"Close your eyes."*

1a. *"Spot a point in the room."*
1b. *"Spot a point in your body."*
1c. *"Find the same point in the room."*
1d. *"Find the same point in your body."*
1e. *"The same point in the room."*
1f. *"The same point in your body."*
  {1e and 1f repeated several times}

2a. *"Spot two points in the room."*
2b. *"Spot two points in your body."*
2c. *"Find the same two points in the room."*
2d. *"Find the same two points in your body."*
2e. *"The same two points in the room."*
2f. *"The same two points in your body."*
  {2e and 2f repeated several times}

3a. *"Spot three points in the room."*
3b. *"Spot three points in your body."*

3c. *"Find the same three points in the room."*

3d. *"Find the same three points in your body."*

3e. *"The same three points in the room."*

3f. *"The same three points in your body."*
{*3e* and *3f* repeated a dozen times}

4a. *"Three points in the room."*

4b. *"Three points outside the building."*
{*4a* and *4b* repeated a dozen times}

5a. *"Wherever you are, whatever you are looking at; make a copy of it."*

5b. *"Make another copy of it; exactly like the first."*

5c. *"And make another copy of it."*

5d. *"And another copy."*

5e. *"Take these copies; pull them together; and push them into the Body."*

5f. *"Whatever you are looking at now; make a copy just like it."*

5g. *"Make another copy of it."*

5h. *"And make another copy of it."*

5i. *"And another copy."*

5j. *"Take these copies; pull them together; and push them into the Body."*

6a. *"Wherever you are, reach your attention to locate a Nothingness."*

6b. *"Make a copy of it."*

6c. *"And make another copy of it."*

6d. *"And another copy."*

6e. *"Take these copies; pull them together; and throw them away in the distance."*

7a. *"Spot a point in space where you are certain you are not."*

7b. *"Spot another place you are not."*

7c. *"Spot two places you are certain you are not."*

7d. *"Spot three places you are not."*

7e. *"Spot three houses you are not in."*

7f. *"Spot three schools you do not attend."*

7g. *"Spot three businesses you do not work for."*

7h. *"Spot three groups you do not belong to."*

7i. *"Spot three animals you are not being."*

7j. *"Spot three planets you are not currently on."*

7k. *"Spot three universes you are not currently in."*

8a. *"Spot a calm space in this Universe."*

8b. *"Spot a calm place in the Body."*
{*8a* and *8b* repeated a couple times}

9a. *"Spot the two back upper corner-points in the room."*

9b. *"Reach your attention and just hold onto those two corner-points."*
{*corner-points* held for two minutes}

10a. *"Sense the chair under the Body."*

10b. *"Sense the floor beneath the feet."*

10c. *"End of Session."*

Your next Advanced Training manual is:
"Mastering Ascension"

BASIC SYSTEMOLOGY GLOSSARY

actualization : to make actual, not just potential; to bring into full solid Reality; to realize fully in *Awareness* as a "thing."

agreement (reality) : unanimity of opinion of what is "thought" to be known; an accepted arrangement of how things are; things we consider as "real" or as an "is" of "reality"; a consensus of what is real as made by standard-issue (common) participants; what an individual contributes to or accepts as "real"; in *Systemology*, a synonym for "*reality.*"

alpha : the first, primary, basic, superior or beginning of some form; in *Systemology*, referring to the state of existence operating on spiritual archetypes and postulates, will and intention "exterior" to the low-level condensation and solidarity of energy and matter as the 'physical universe' (*beta*).

alpha-spirit : a "spiritual" *Life*-form; the "true" *Self* or I-AM; the *individual*; the spiritual (*alpha*) *Self* that is animating the (*beta*) physical body or "*genetic vehicle*" using a continuous *Lifeline* of spiritual ("*ZU*") energy; an individual spiritual (*alpha*) entity possessing no physical

114

mass or measurable waveform (motion) in the Physical Universe as itself, so it animates the (*beta*) physical body or "*genetic vehicle*" as a catalyst to experience *Self*-determined causality in effect within the *Physical Universe*; a singular unit or point of *Spiritual Awareness* that is *Aware* that it is *Aware*.

alpha thought : the highest spiritual *Self-determination* over creation and existence exercised by an Alpha-Spirit; the Alpha range of pure *Creative Ability* based on direct postulates and considerations of *Beingness*; spiritual qualities comparable to "thought" but originating in Alpha-existence, independently superior to a Mind-System.

ascension : actualized *Awareness* elevated to the point of true "spiritual existence" exterior to *beta existence*. An "Ascended Master" is one who has returned to an incarnation on Earth as an inherently *Enlightened One*, demonstrable in their words and actions; they have the ability to *Self-direct* the "Mind" and "Body" as *Self* (as a "Spirit"); and to maintain consciousness as a personal identity continuum with the same *Self-directed* control and communication of Will-Intention that is exercised, actualized and developed deliberately during one's present incarnation.

associative knowledge : significance or meaning of a facet or aspect assigned to (or considered to have) a direct relationship with another facet; to connect or relate ideas or facets of existence with one another; in traditional systems logic, an equivalency of significance or meaning between facets or sets that are grouped together, such as in *(a + b) + c = a + (b + c)*; in Systemology, erroneous associative knowledge is assignment of the same value to all facets or parts considered as related (even when they are not actually so), such as in *a = a, b = a, c = a* and so forth without distinction.

attention : active use of *Awareness* toward a specific aspect or thing; the act of "attending" with the presence of *Self*; a direction of focus or concentration of *Awareness* along a particular channel or conduit or toward a particular terminal node or communication termination point; the Self-directed concentration of personal energy as a combination of observation, thought-waves and consideration; focused application of *Self-Directed Awareness*.

awareness : the highest sense of-and-as *Self* in knowing and being as I-AM (the *Alpha-Spirit*); the extent of beingness directed as a viewpoint (POV) experienced by *Self* as *Knowingness*.

beta (awareness) : all consciousness activity ("*Awareness*") in the "Physical Universe" (KI,

116

in *Zuism*) or else in *beta-existence*; *Awareness* within the range of the *genetic-body*, including material thoughts, emotional responses and physical motors; personal *Awareness* of physical energy and physical matter moving through physical space and experienced as "time"; the *Awareness* held by *Self* that is restricted to an organic *Lifeform* or "*genetic vehicle*" in which it experiences causality in *beta-existence*.

beta (existence) : all manifestation in the "Physical Universe" (KI, in *Zuism*); the conditions of *Awareness* for the *Alpha-spirit* (*Self*) as a physical organic *Lifeform* or "*genetic vehicle*" in which it experiences causality in the *Physical Universe*.

charge : to fill or furnish with a quality; to supply with energy; to lay a command upon; in *Systemology*—to imbue with intention; to overspread with emotion; personal energy stores and significances entwined as fragmentation in mental images, reactive-response encoding and intellectual (and/or) programmed beliefs.

channel : a specific stream, course, current, direction or route; to form or cut a groove or ridge or otherwise guide along a specific course; a direct path; an artificial aqueduct created to connect two water bodies or water or make travel possible.

circuit : a circular path or loop; a closed-path within a system that allows a flow; a pattern or action or wave movement that follows a specific route or potential path only; in *Systemology*, "*communication processing*" pertaining to a specific *flow* of energy or information along a channel; "*feedback loop.*"

communication : successful transmission of information, data, energy (&tc.) along a message line, with a reception of feedback; an energetic flow of intention to cause an effect (or duplication) at a distance; the personal energy moved or acted upon by will or else 'selective directed attention'; the 'messenger action' used to transmit and receive energy across a medium; also relay of energy, a message or signal—or even locating a personal POV (viewpoint) for the Self—along the *ZU-line*.

condense (condensation) : the transition of vapor to liquid; denoting a change in state to a more substantial or solid condition; leading to a more compact or solid form.

confront : to come around in front of; to be in the presence of; to stand in front of, or in the face of; to meet "face-to-face" or "face-up-to"; additionally, in *Systemology*, to fully tolerate or acceptably withstand an encounter with a particular manifestation without an automatic reactive response.

118

consideration : careful analytical reflection of all aspects; deliberation; determining the significance of a "thing" in relation to similarity or dissimilarity to other "things"; evaluation of facts and importance of certain facts; thorough examination of all aspects related to, or important for, making a decision; the analysis of consequences and estimation of significance when making decisions; also in *Systemology*, the *postulate* or *Alpha-Thought* that defines the state of *beingness* for what something "*is.*"

defragmentation : the *reparation* of wholeness; collecting all dispersed parts to reform an original whole; a process of removing "*fragmentation*" in data or knowledge to provide a clear understanding; applying techniques and processes that promote a *holistic* interconnected *alpha* state, favoring observational *Awareness* of continuity in all spiritual and physical systems; in *Systemology*, a "*Seeker*" achieving actualized "*Self-Honest Awareness*" is said to be in a basic state of *beta-defragmentation*, whereas *Alpha-defragmentation* is the rehabilitation of the *creative ability*, managing the *Spiritual Timeline* and the POV of *Self* as Alpha-Spirit (I-AM).

existence : the *state* or fact of *apparent manifestation*; the resulting combination of the Principles of Manifestation: consciousness, motion and substance; continued *survival*; that which independently exists.

exterior : outside of; on the outside; in *Systemology*, we mean specifically the POV of *Self* that is *'outside of'* the *Human Condition,* free of the physical and mental trappings of the Physical Universe; a metahuman range of consideration; see also *'Zu-Vision'*.

external : a force coming from outside; information received from outside sources; in *Systemology*, the objective *'Physical Universe'* existence, or *beta-existence*, that the Physical Body or *genetic vehicle* is essentially *anchored* to for its considerations of locational space-time as a dimension or POV.

fragmentation : breaking into parts and scattering the pieces; the *fractioning* of wholeness or the *fracture* of a holistic interconnected *alpha* state, favoring observational *Awareness* of perceived connectivity between parts; *discontinuity*; separation of a totality into parts; in *Systemology*, a person outside of *Self-Honesty* is said to be operating from a *fragmented* state.

flow : movement across (or through) a channel (or conduit); a direction of active energetic motion, typically distinguished as either an *in-flow*, *out-flow* or *cross-flow*.

genetic-vehicle : a physical *Life*-form; the physical (*beta*) body that is animated/controlled by the (*Alpha*) *Spirit* using a continuous *Spiritual Lifeline* (ZU); a physical (*beta*) organic receptacle and catalyst for the (*Alpha*) *Self* to operate "causes" and experience "effects" within the *Physical Universe*.

harmful-act : a counter-survival mode of behavior or action (esp. that causes harm to one of more *Spheres of Existence*)—or—an overtly aggressive (hostile and/or destructive) action against an individual or any other *Sphere of Existence*; in *Utilitarian Systemology*—a shortsighted (serves fewest/lowest *Spheres of Existence*) intentional overtly harmful action to resolve a perceived problem; a revision of the rule for standard *Utilitarianism* for Systemology to distinguish actions which provide the least benefit to the least number of *Spheres of Existence*, or else the greatest harm to the greatest number of *Spheres of Existence*; in *moral philosophy*—an action which can be experienced by few and/or which one would not be willing to experience for themselves (*theft, slander, rape, &tc*); an iniquity or iniquitous act.

hold-back : withheld communications (esp. actions) such as "*Hold-Outs*"; intentional (or automatic) withdrawal (as opposed to reach); Self-restraint (which may eventually be enforced or automated); not reaching, acting or expressing, when one should be; an ability that is now restrained (on automatic) due to inability to withhold it on Self-determinism alone.

hold-outs : in photography, the numerous snapshots/pictures withheld from the final display or professional presentation of the event; withheld communications; in Utilitarian Systemology—energetic withdrawal and communication breaks with a "*terminal*" and its *Sphere of Existence* as a result of a "*Harmful-Act*"; unspoken or undiscovered (hidden, covert) actions that an individual withholds communications of, fearing punishment or endangerment of *Self-preservation* (*First Sphere*); the act of hiding (or keeping hidden) the truth of a "*Harmful-Act*"; a refusal to communicate with a *Pilot*; also "*Hold-Back.*"

holistic : the examination of interconnected systems as encompassing something greater than the *sum* of their "parts."

Human Condition : a standard default state of Human experience that is generally accepted to be the extent of its potential identity (*beingness*) —currently treated as *Homo Sapiens Sapiens,* but which is scheduled for replacement by *Homo Novus* (the "New Human").

imagination : ability to create *mental imagery* in one's Personal Universe at will and change or alter it as desired; the ability to create, change and dissolve mental images on command or as an act of will; to create a mental image or have associated imagery displayed (or "conjured") in the mind that may or may not be treated as real (or memory recall) and may or may not accurately duplicate objective reality; to employ *creative abilities* of the Spirit that are independent of reality agreements with beta-existence.

imprint : to strongly impress, stamp, mark (or outline) onto a softer 'impressible' substance; to mark with pressure onto a surface; in *Systemology*, used to indicate permanent Reality impressions marked by frequencies, energies or interactions experienced during periods of emotional distress, pain, unconsciousness, loss, enforcement, or something antagonistic to physical (personal) survival, all of which are are stored with other reactive response-mechanisms at lower-levels of *Awareness* as opposed to the active memory database and proactive processing center of the Mind; an experiential "memory-set" that may later resurface—be triggered or stimulated artificially—as Reality, of which similar responses will be engaged automatically; holographic-like imagery "stamped" onto consciousness as composed of energetic *facets* tied to the "snap-shot" of an experience.

imprinting incident : the first or original event

instance communicated and *emotionally encoded* onto an individual's "*Spiritual Timeline*" (recorded memory from all lifetimes), which formed a permanent impression that is later used to mechanistically treat future contact on that channel; the first or original occurrence of some particular *facet* or mental image related to a certain type of *encoded response*, such as pain and discomfort, losses and victimization, and even the acts that we have taken against others along the *Spiritual Timeline* of our existence that caused them to also be *Imprinted*.

intention : directed application of Will; to intend (have "in Mind") or signify (give "significance" to) for or toward a particular purpose; in *Systemology* (from the *Standard Model*)—the spiritual activity at WILL (5.0) directed by an *Alpha Spirit* (7.0); the application of WILL as "Cause" from a higher order of Alpha Thought and consideration (6.0).

interior : inside of; on the inside; in *Systemology*, we mean specifically the POV of *Self* that is fixed to the *'internal' Human Condition,* including the *Reactive Control Center* (RCC) and Mind-System or *Master Control Center* (MCC); within *beta-existence*.

internal : a force coming from inside; information received from inside sources; in *Systemology*, the objective experience of *beta-existence*

124

associated with the Physical Body or *genetic vehicle* and its POV regarding sensation and perception; from inside the body; in the body.

invalidate : decrease the level or degree or *agreement* as Reality.

mental image : a subjectively experienced "picture" created and imagined into being by the Alpha-Spirit (or at lower levels, one of its automated mechanisms) that includes all perceptible *facets* of totally immersive scene, which may be forms originated by an individual, or a "facsimile-copy" ("snap-shot") of something seen or encountered; a duplication of wave-forms in one's Personal Universe as a "picture" that mirror an "external" Universe experience, such as an *Imprint*.

perception : internalized processing of data received by the *senses*; to become *Aware of* via the senses.

pilot : a professional steersman responsible for healthy functional operation of a ship toward a specific destination; in *Systemology*, an intensive trained individual qualified to specially apply *Systemology Processing* to assist other *Seekers* on the *Pathway*.

point-of-view (POV) : a point to view from; an opinion or attitude as expressed from a specific identity-phase; a specific standpoint or vantage-point; a definitive manner of consideration specific to an individual phase or identity; a place or position affording a specific view or vantage; circumstances and programming of an individual that is conducive to a particular response, consideration or belief-set (paradigm); a position (consideration) or place (location) that provides a specific view or perspective (subjective) on experience (of the objective).

postulate : to put forward as truth; to suggest or assume an existence *to be*; to state or affirm the existence of particular conditions; to provide a basis of reasoning and belief; a basic theory accepted as fact; in *Systemology*, Alpha-Thought —the top-most decisions or considerations made by the Alpha-Spirit regarding the "*is-ness*" (what things "are") about energy-matter and space-time.

presence : a quality of some thing (*energy/matter*) being "present" in space-time; personal orientation of *Self* as an *Awareness* (*POV*) located in present space-time (environment) and communicating with extant energy-matter.

processing command line (PCL) : a directed input; a specific command using highly selective language for *Systemology Processing*; a predetermined directive statement (cause) intended to focus concentrated attention (effect).

processing, systematic : the inner-workings or "through-put" result of systems; in *Systemology*, a method of applied spiritual technology used toward personal Self-Actualization; methods of selective directed attention, communicated language and associative imagery that increases personal control of the human condition.

realization : the clear perception of an understanding; a consideration or understanding on what is "actual"; to make "real" or give "reality" to so as to grant a property of "beingness" or "being as it is"; the state or instance of coming to an *Awareness*; in *Systemology*, "gnosis" or true knowledge achieved during *systematic processing*; achievement of a new (or higher) cognition, true knowledge or perception of Self; a consideration of reality or assignment of meaning.

responsibility : the *ability* to *respond*; the extent of mobilizing *power* and *understanding* an individual maintains as *Awareness* to enact *change*; the proactive ability to *Self-direct* and make decisions independent of an outside authority.

Seeker : an individual on the *Pathway to Self-Honesty*; a practitioner of *Mardukite Systemology* or *Systemology Processing*, that is working toward *Spiritual Ascension*.

Self-actualization : bringing the full potential of the Human spirit into Reality; expressing full capabilities and creativeness of the *Alpha-Spirit*.

Self-determinism : the freedom to act, clear of external control or influence; the personal control of Will to direct intention.

Self-honesty : the basic or original *alpha* state of *being* and *knowing*; clear and present total *Awareness* of-and-as *Self*, in its most basic and true proactive expression of itself as *Spirit* or *I-AM*—free of artificial attachments, perceptive filters and other emotionally-reactive or mentally-conditioned programming imposed on the human condition by the systematized physical world; the ability to experience existence without judgment.

spiritual timeline : a continuous stream of moment-to-moment *Mental Images* (or a record of experiences) that defines the "past" of a spiritual being (or *Alpha-Spirit*) and which includes impressions (*imprints, &tc.*) from all life-incarnations and significant spiritual events the being has encountered; in Systemology, also "*backtrack.*"

Spheres of Existence : a series of *eight* concentric circles, rings or spheres (each larger than the former) that is overlaid onto the Standard Model of Beta-Existence to demonstrate the dynamic systems of existence extending out from the POV of Self (often as a "body") at the *First Sphere*; these are given in the basic eightfold systems as: *Self*, *Home/Family*, *Groups*, *Humanity*, *Life on Earth*, *Physical Universe*, *Spiritual Universe* and *Infinity-Divinity.*

Systemology : a modern tradition of applied religious philosophy and spiritual technology based on *Arcane Tablets* (in combination with "*general systemology*" and "*games theory*") developed in the New Age underground by Joshua Free in 2011 as an advanced futurist extension of the *Mardukite Research Org.*

terminal (node) : a point, end, or mass, on a line; a connection point for closing an electric circuit, such as a post on a battery terminating at each end of its own systematic function; a point of connectivity with other points; in systems, a contact point of interaction; a point of interaction with other points.

turbulence : a quality or state of distortion or disturbance that creates irregularity of a flow or pattern; the quality or state of aberration on a line (such as ragged edges) or the emotional "turbulent feelings" attached to a particular flow or terminal node; a violent, haphazard or disharmonious commotion (such as in the ebb of gusts and lulls of wind action).

validation : a reinforcement of agreements or considerations as being "real."

viewpoint : see *"point-of-view" (POV)*.

willingness : the state of conscious Self-determined ability and interest (directed attention) to *Be, Do* or *Have*; a Self-determined consideration to reach, face up to (*confront*) or manage some "mass" or energy; the extent to which an individual considers themselves able to participate, act or communicate along some line, to put attention or intention on the line, or to produce (create) an effect.

ZU : the ancient Sumerian cuneiform sign for the archaic verb—*"to know," "knowingness"* or *"awareness"*; in *Mardukite Zuism and Systemology*, the active energy/matter of the "Spiritual Universe" (AN) experienced as a *Lifeforce* or *consciousness* that imbues living forms extant in the "Physical Universe" (KI); *"Spiritual Life Energy"*; energy demonstrated by the WILL of an actualized *Alpha-Spirit* in the "Spiritual Universe" (AN), which impinges its *Awareness* into the Physical Universe (KI), animating/controlling *Life* for its experience of *beta-existence* along an individual Alpha-Spirit's personal *Identity-continuum*, called a *ZU-line*.

***Zu*-Line** : a theoretical construct in *Mardukite Zuism and Systemology* demonstrating *Spiritual*

130

Life Energy (ZU) as a personal individual "continuum" of Awareness interacting with all Spheres of Existence on the Standard Model of Systemology; a spectrum of potential variations and interactions of a monistic continuum or singular *Spiritual Life Energy* demonstrated on the Standard Model; an energetic channel of potential POV and "locations" of Beingness, demonstrated in early Systemology materials as an individual Alpha-Spirit's personal *Identity- continuum*, potentially connecting *Awareness* of *Self* with "*Infinity*" simultaneous with all points considered in existence; a symbolic demonstration of the "*Life-line*" on which *Awareness (ZU)* extends from the direction of the "Spiritual Universe" (AN) in its true original *alpha state* through an entire possible range of activity resulting in its *beta state* and control of a *genetic-entity* occupying the *Physical Universe (KI)*.

Zu-Vision : the true and basic (*Alpha*) Point-of-View (perspective, POV) maintained by *Self* as *Alpha-Spirit* outside boundaries or considerations of the *Human Condition* and *exterior* to beta-existence reality agreements with the Physical Universe; a POV of Self *as* "a unit of Spiritual Awareness" that exists independent of a "body" and entrapment in a *Human Condition*; "spirit vision" in its truest sense.

Collector's Edition Hardcover

THE FUNDAMENTALS OF
SYSTEMOLOGY

A Basic Course developed by
Joshua Free

*collecting material of six lesson-booklets
together in one volume!*

"Being More Than Human"

"Realities in Agreement"

"Windows To Experience"

"Ancient Systemology"

"A History of Systemology"

"Systemology Processing"

All *six* lesson-booklets of the first official
Basic Course on Mardukite Systemology
are combined together in *one volume* as
"Fundamentals of Systemology."

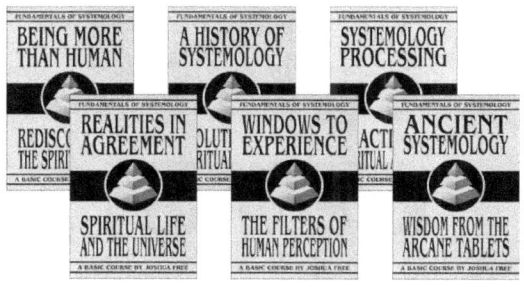

Lesson booklets are also available individually!

Collector's Edition Hardcover

THE PATHWAY TO

ASCENSION

The Official 2024 Systemology
Professional Course by
Joshua Free

All sixteen lessons available in two volumes!

"Increasing Awareness"

"Thought & Emotion"

"Clear Communication"

"Handling Humanity"

"Free Your Spirit"

"Escaping Spirit-Traps"

"Eliminating Barriers"

"Conquest of Illusion"

All *sixteen* lesson-booklets of the newest
Professional Course on Mardukite Systemology
are combined together in *two volumes* as
"The Pathway to Ascension."

Lesson booklets are also available individually!

Collector's Edition Hardcover

KEYS TO THE

KINGDOM

The Official Systemology
Advanced Training Course by
Joshua Free

All eight A.T. manuals available in two volumes!

"The Secret of Universes"

"Games, Goals and Purposes"

"The Jewel of Knowledge"

"Implanted Universes"

"Entities and Fragments"

"Spiritual Perception"

"Mastering Ascension"

"Advancing Systemology"

All *eight* A.T. manuals of the *New Standard*
Systemology *Advanced Training Course*
along with *three* training supplements
are combined together
in *two volumes* as
"Keys to the Kingdom."

Manuals are also available as individual booklets!

THE SYSTEM

Seekers and students of the *Professional Course* and *Advanced Training Course* will also be interested in the original *Systemology Core Research Series*. These 8 volumes are a complete chronological record of *Mardukite NexGen New Thought* developments published by the *Systemology Society* from 2019 through 2023.

The Systemology Core series begins with the first professional publication released when our *Mardukite Systemology* emerged from the underground in 2019, with: *"The Tablets of Destiny Revelation."*

OLOGY CORE

The Tablets of Destiny Revelation:
*How Long-Lost Anunnaki Wisdom
Can Change the Fate of Humanity*

Crystal Clear: *Handbook for Seekers*

Metahuman Destinations (*2 volumes*)

Imaginomicon:
Approaching Gateways to Higher Universes

Way of the Wizard: *Utilitarian Systemology*

Systemology-180: *Fast-Track to Ascension*

Systemology Backtrack:
Reclaiming Spiritual Power & Past-Life Memory

PUBLISHED BY THE **JOSHUA FREE** IMPRINT REPRESENTING

The Mardukite Academy of Systemology

mardukite.com

www.ingramcontent.com/pod-product-compliance
Lightning Source LLC
Chambersburg PA
CBHW071156120626
46546CB00006B/2292